This edition first published in 1993 by
Sunburst Books, Deacon House, 65 Old Church Street,
London, SW3 5BS

Copyright © Editorial LIBSA, Narciso Serra, 25 – Tel 433 54 07 –
28007 MADRID
4.ª EDICION 1991
Copyright English language text © 1993 Sunburst Books

ISBN 1 85778 006 X

Printed and bound in China

DESSERTS
AND PASTRIES

CONTENTS

INTRODUCTION

For many people the sweet tooth is always the most predominant, and savouries take second place to cakes, puddings and sweets.

No matter how many courses you have served at lunch or dinner there will always be takers for pudding or something sweet to round off the meal. Of course these expectations can be fulfilled by some grapes or fresh peaches or strawberries – simplicity itself – but they can definitely be exceeded by a pudding or cake.

Desserts and Pastries provides a range of recipes for every type of occasion where something sweet is required, from simple fruit puddings such as Bananas Flambé to more exotic preparations like Chestnut Charlotte, as well as numerous recipes for cakes, pastries, biscuits and sweets.

This book has been divided into three sections – Desserts, Cakes and Flans, & Pastries, Biscuits and Sweets – to make it as easy as possible for the reader to select the type of recipe which is most appropriate for a specific occasion.

Left: Cadiz-style Turron
(recipe on page 60)
Fruit Turron
Right: (recipe on page 60)

DESSERTS

FRUIT ICE-CREAM

Serves 6-8

Ice-cream:
250g/8oz canned fruit in syrup
4 eggs, separated
250g/8oz caster sugar
2 tbsp icing sugar
450ml/³/4 pint double or whipping cream

Blackcurrant Sauce:
350g/12 oz blackcurrant jelly or jam
juice of ¹/2 lemon
100ml/4 fl oz water

For a 20.5cm x 7.5cm/8in x 3in round mould
or a 25.5cm/10in long oblong mould

Drain the fruit and reserve 75ml/3fl oz of the syrup. Chop the fruit finely and marinate in the reserved syrup for 30 minutes.

Beat together the egg yolks and caster sugar until creamy then add the fruit. Beat the egg whites with the icing sugar until stiff peaks form. In a separate bowl, beat the cream until stiff. Carefully fold the beaten egg whites into the fruit mixture. Pour onto the cream and mix together. Pour into a lightly greased mould and freeze overnight.

Turn out the ice-cream by dipping the mould in hot water for a moment. Serve with the warm blackcurrant sauce.

To make the blackcurrant sauce, combine all the ingredients together and heat gently.

PEACH CROWN

Serves 6-8

4 egg whites
250g/8oz caster sugar
1 tbsp white wine
few drops of vanilla essence
¹/2 tsp cream of tartar
1 medium can peaches, drained
¹/2 litre/³/4 pint double or whipping cream
Fresh or canned cherries to decorate

Beat the egg whites until stiff then gradually beat in the sugar with the vinegar, vanilla essence and cream of tartar.

Place the mixture in a piping bag fitted with a large plain nozzle and pipe 12 rings onto a baking sheet lined with greased greaseproof paper. Bake in the oven at 150°C/300°F/Gas Mark 2 for 1¹/2 hours. Turn onto a wire rack, peel off the paper and leave to cool.

Arrange the meringues in a circle on a serving dish. Top each one with a peach half. Beat the cream until stiff then pipe through a fluted nozzle onto the peaches. Decorate with cherries and serve well chilled. Ice cream may be used instead of whipped cream.

CHESTNUT DELIGHT

Serves 6-8

1kg/2.2lbs chestnuts, cooked and peeled
1kg/2.2lbs sugar
200ml/7fl oz water
150ml/¹/4 pint double or whipping cream

Place the cooked chestnuts in a liquidizer or food processor and blend to a purée.

Put the purée in a saucepan with the sugar and water and heat gently until the sugar dissolves. Increase the heat and simmer for 15 minutes, stirring continuously until the mixture becomes a syrup. Remove from the heat and leave to cool. Serve on small glass dessert plates, if possible, decorated with whipped cream.

QUINCE SWEETMEAT

Serves 6-8

12 large quinces, peeled, cored and chopped
the equivalent weight in sugar

Place the chopped quinces in a saucepan with a little water, cover and cook gently until soft. Purée the pulp in a blender or food processor and return to the pan. Add the sugar and cook for 30-35 minutes, stirring frequently.

Pour the mixture into lightly greased ramekin dishes, chill well then turn out to serve.

MANDARIN CHARLOTTE RUSSE

Serves 4

125g/4oz packet lemon jelly
300g/10oz canned mandarin oranges
18 sponge fingers
300ml/¹/2 pint double or whipping cream
15g/¹/2 oz crystallised angelica, chopped
1-2 tbsp Curacao, Grand Marnier or Cointreau
Whipped cream and mandarin segments to decorate

Wet the inside of a 600ml/1 pint pudding basin with water.

Dissolve the jelly in 300ml/¹/2 pint of boiling water, and add the juice from the can of mandarin oranges to make up 450ml/³/4 pint of liquid.

Pour enough of the jelly mixture into the basin to coat the bottom and refrigerate until the jelly is set. Soak the sponge fingers in the liquid jelly and use to line the basin, rounded end uppermost.

Make a pattern with some mandarin segments on the jelly in the bottom of the basin, then arrange the chopped angelica, moistened with liquid jelly, in between. Refrigerate to firm up the sponge fingers and mandarin pattern.

Pour another coat of jelly on top, and chill well.

Meanwhile, whip the cream and stir in the liqueur. Fill the centre of the mould with alternate layers of cream and mandarin segments, finishing with cream. Pour the rest of the jelly mixture onto the sponge fingers around the sides of the basin until they are well soaked. Do not add any more once the liquid has reached the rim of the basin. Chill well overnight.

Turn out onto a serving dish. The easiest way to turn out the charlotte is to dip the basin in boiling water for a few first. Decorate with whipped cream and mandarin segments, if desired.

Top: Quince Sweetmeat
Bottom: Mandarin Charlotte Russe

CREAMY CUSTARD WITH SPUN SUGAR

Serves 8

10 tbsp sugar
1 litre/1¾ pints milk
4 eggs
1 tbsp cornflour
1 sponge finger

For the spun sugar
3 tbsp sugar
Squeeze of lemon

Heat 4 tablespoons of the sugar in a saucepan until caramelised. In a separate pan, heat the milk to boiling point and pour onto the caramel immediately. Leave to dissolve.

Meanwhile whisk the eggs with the cornflour and remaining sugar. Bring the caramelised milk to boiling point again, add the egg mixture and stir continuously over the heat until it thickens. Allow to cool, stirring from time to time to prevent a skin forming.

When the custard is cold, pour into a deep glass dish, and place a sponge finger in the middle on top - this will serve to support the spun sugar.

Spun sugar. Place the sugar and lemon juice in a heavy-based saucepan and heat until the sugar dissolves. Increase the heat and cook until caramelised. Remove the pan from the heat and stir with a wooden spoon until fine strands start to form in the caramel. Dip 2 wooden spoons in the caramel and start to put them together and pull them apart, moving the spoons slowly so that strands of spun sugar form between them. As you are working, batches of the spun sugar can be round around 2 forks stuck in uncooked potatoes to stand upright. When all the caramel is turned into spun sugar, place the sugar carefully on top of the sponge fingers in the custard dish, and against the sides. Do not allow the spun sugar to touch the custard or it will dissolve.

SPANISH CHRISTMAS PANTOMIME PUDDING

Serves 10

250g/8oz dried peaches or apricots, sliced
250g/8oz dried figs
100g/4oz raisins
150ml/5 fl oz port
250g/½ lb prunes
100ml/4 fl oz water
3 cloves
100g/4oz walnuts
juice of 1 orange
grated rind and juice of 1 lemon
500g/1lb Golden Delicious apples
500g/1lb pears, peeled, cored and quartered
pinch of nutmeg

Soak the dried fruit in the port.

Make a syrup with the water and sugar, then add the cloves, walnuts, orange juice, lemon rind and juice. Cook for 5 minutes, then remove the cloves.

Drain the dried fruit, reserving the port. Add the dried fruit, fresh fruit and nutmeg to the syrup and simmer for 30 minutes until all the fruit and nuts are tender. Add the port.

Remove 2 or 3 prunes, 1 dried apricot and 2 pieces of apple and place in a blender. Liquidize to a purée and use to thicken the sauce.

Serve chilled with a topping of chopped walnuts and single or whipped cream.

ANGEL HAIR

Serves 6

2kg/4½ lbs pumpkin or squash
Sugar (see recipe)
pinch of cinnamon
grated rind of 1 lemon

Cut the pumpkin or squash into large slices, then remove and discard the seeds and fibres. Place the slices in a saucepan with enough cold water to cover. Cover and simmer for 1 hour. Remove and discard the skin and rinse the pulp thoroughly in running water. Wrap the pulp in a muslin cloth and press hard to squeeze out the moisture. Weigh the pulp and place in a saucepan. Measure the same weight in sugar and add to the pan with the cinnamon and grated rind and juice of the lemon. Cover and simmer for 30-35 minutes. Pour into preserving jars and seal.

COFFEE ICE-CREAM

Serves 8

4 eggs
9 tbsp icing sugar
2 tbsp strong black coffee
600ml/1 pint double cream, whipped

To decorate:
Chocolate coffee beans
Whipped cream

Mix the sugar with the coffee.

Whisk the eggs until frothy. Add the coffee mixture and carefully blend in the cream.

Pour into a cake tin greased with butter and freeze for 12 hours.

To turn it out, dip the container in hot water for a few moments.

STUFFED PINEAPPLE

Serves 8

1 Pineapple - 1kg/2.2 lbs
500g/1lb strawberries
9 tbsp sugar
75ml/3 fl oz Kirsch
3 eggs, separated
Icing sugar

Cut the pineapple in half lengthways. Remove the pulp and dice it, collecting any juice that drips out. Slice the strawberries, and mix them with the pineapple dice.

Add 3 tablespoons of the sugar to the Kirsch, pour over the fruit, leave to marinate for 30 minutes, then drain well, reserving the juices. Place the egg yolks and 3 tablespoons of the sugar in a mixing bowl placed over a pan of simmering water. Beat well together then add the reserved fruit juices and heat the mixture until it thickens.

Fill the pineapple halves with the fruit and pour the sauce over the top. Beat the egg whites with the remaining sugar until very stiff. Fill a piping bag with the mixture and pipe onto the pineapple halves. Dust with icing sugar and bake in the oven at 230°C/450°F/Gas Mark 8 for about 10 minutes until the topping is golden.

Top: Spanish Christmas Pantomime Pudding
Bottom: Stuffed Pineapple

ORANGE PUDDING

Serves 6

50g/2oz currants
75ml/3 fl oz brandy
50g/2 oz granulated sugar
100ml /4 fl oz milk
250g/8oz French bread, sliced
1 jar orange marmalade
4 eggs, beaten
50g/2oz butter
4 tbsp caster sugar
2 tbsp water

Soak the currants in the brandy for at least 2 hours. Drain and reserve the brandy. Place the granulated sugar and milk in a saucepan and bring to the boil. Add the bread slices and stir over a low heat until the bread has completely disintegrated.

Remove from the heat and add the marmalade and currants, then add the beaten eggs, butter and brandy.

Heat the caster sugar and water together until caramelised then use to coat the base and sides of a savarin tin. Pour the bread mixture into the tin and bake in a bain-marie in the oven at 200°C/400°F/Gas Mark 6 for 40 minutes. Turn out while still hot.

ORANGE AND PINEAPPLE MERINGUES

Serves 6

6 oranges
1 small can pineapple slices
3 eggs, separated
1 tbsp melted butter
75ml/3 fl oz Curacao
6 tbsp sugar

Cut the oranges in half, carefully remove the flesh and reserve the shells. Chop the orange flesh and pineapple pieces.

Beat the egg yolks with the butter and half the sugar until frothy. Add the Curacao and the fruit and stir well. Pour the mixture into the orange shells.

Beat the egg whites with the remaining sugar until very stiff. Spoon or pip the whites onto the orange shells and bake in the oven at 230°C/450°F/Gas Mark 8 for a few minutes.

BAKED APPLES IN PUFF PASTRY

Serves 6

500g/1lb puff pastry
6 medium-sized apples, peeled and cored
1 egg white
1/2 jar raspberry jam
juice of 1/2 lemon
1 egg, beaten
icing sugar

Roll out the puff pastry to 1/2 mm/1/4 inch thickness and cut into long narrow strips. Wind the strips around the apples starting at the base and working upwards in a spiral. Seal the edges and ends with egg white.

Place the apples in an ovenproof dish. Mix together the raspberry jam and lemon juice and fill the apples with this mixture. Cover the top with a puff pastry decoration and brush with beaten egg. Bake in the oven at 230°C/450°F/Gas Mark 8 for 25–30 minutes. When the pastry is golden, remove and serve hot, dusted with icing sugar.

Accompany with whipped cream and a caramel sauce if liked.

Left: Baked Apples in Puff Pastry
Opposite, top: Orange and Pinapple Meringue
Opposite, bottom: Orange Pudding

MERINGUE MUSHROOMS

Serves 6

4 egg whites
250g/8oz icing sugar
6 servings ice-cream
1/2 tsp cinnamon
100g/4oz chocolate

To make the meringue, place the egg whites and sugar in a mixing bowl over a pan of simmering water. Whisk slowly to combine then whisk rapidly until the mixture is thick and creamy. Remove the bowl from the heat and continue whisking for 5 minutes. Pipe mushroom shapes onto a baking tray lined with greaseproof paper, making half the mushrooms a smaller size. Leave overnight to dry out. Sandwich the ice-cream between 2 meringues, using a smaller one as the base. Dust with cinnamon and serve in a pool of melted chocolate.

ORANGE SOUFFLÉ

Serves 6

1/2 litre/3/4 pint milk
25g/1oz melted butter
4 egg yolks
6 egg whites
25g/1oz cornflour
grated rind of 2 oranges
100ml/4 fl oz orange juice
few drops of Cointreau

Make a custard sauce, following the instructions given in the recipe for Apple Tart with Blackberry Sauce on page 40. Add the orange juice and rind.

When the sauce has cooled slightly, add the butter, the egg yolks and the cornflour and mix thoroughly. Beat the egg whites until stiff and fold in.

Place in a soufflé dish greased with butter and dusted with sugar and bake for 30 minutes in the oven at 180°C/350°F/Gas Mark 4. Dust with caster sugar and serve immediately.

CREME CARAMEL

Serves 6

1/2 litre/3/4 pint milk
5 eggs, beaten
5 tbsp caster sugar
100g/4oz granulated sugar
150ml/1/4 pint water

Heat the milk until lukewarm. Beat the eggs and caster sugar together and add the milk.

Place the granulated sugar and water in a saucepan and simmer until a golden caramel colour. Use to coat 600ml/1 pint mould. Strain the custard into the mould, place in a bain-marie and bake in the oven at 180°C/350°F/gas mark 4 for about 45 minutes until set. Allow to cool then turn out and garnish with whipped cream and cherries, if desired.

QUICK CARAMEL CUSTARD

Serves 6

1 medium sized can condensed milk
3 eggs, lightly beaten

Place the condensed milk in a heavy-based saucepan. Measure double the volume in water (using the can) and add to the pan. Simmer until reduced by half. Remove from the heat and allow to cool slightly then add the beaten eggs, mixing thoroughly. Pour into a caramel-coated mould and bake in a bain-marie as for "Creme Caramel", but the custard requires a much shorter cooking time. Turn out and garnish as for "Creme Caramel"

APRICOT SOUFFLÉ

Serves 4

300g/10oz ripe apricots, stoned
Sugar to taste
40g/1 1/2oz butter
40g/1 1/2oz flour
3 egg yolks
1 tbsp lemon juice
4 egg whites

Apricot Sauce:
1 jar apricot jam
2 tbsp sugar
75ml/3fl oz brandy
75ml 3fl oz single cream

Purée the apricots in a liquidizer or food processor. Add sugar to taste - the quantity will vary depending on the acidity of the fruit.

Grease a 15cm/6 inch soufflé dish and wrap 2 layers of greaseproof paper around the outside, allowing about 8cm/13 inches extra at the top. Tie some string around the dish to hold the paper in place and lightly grease the dish.

Melt the butter in a saucepan, gradually add the flour, and cook for 1 minute. Pour in the apricot purée and cook for 5 minutes, stirring continuously. Taste and add more sugar if necessary. Then remove from the heat and allow to cool slightly. Add the egg yolks one at a time, then the lemon juice.

Beat the egg whites until fairly stiff and fold them into the apricot mixture carefully. Pour into the prepared dish and bake in the oven at 190°C/375°F/Gas Mark 5 for about 1 hour. Serve the soufflé hot from the oven topped with the apricot sauce.

For the sauce: heat the apricot jam together with the sugar and brandy to make a smooth sauce, then mix in the cream.

Top: Meringue Mushrooms
Bottom: Orange Soufflé

CUSTARD PUDDING WITH MERINGUES

Serves 6

1 litre / 1³/₄ pints milk
strip of lemon rind
6 eggs, separated
8 tbsp sugar plus 6 tbsp sugar (for the meringues)
1 tbsp cornflour
few drops of vanilla essence

Place the milk in a saucepan with the lemon rind and bring to the boil. Place the egg yolks, sugar and cornflour in a mixing bowl placed over a pan of simmering water. Beat well until light and frothy. Gradually add the hot milk, stirring constantly. Continue cooking until the mixture thickens and becomes creamy, then add the vanilla essence. Remove from the heat and allow to cool, stirring occasionally to prevent a skin forming on the surface.

Beat the egg-whites with the rest of the sugar until very stiff for the meringue balls. Place small round portions of the mixture onto a baking tray and bake in the oven at 230°C/450°F/gas mark 8 for a few minutes.

When the custard cream is cold, serve in bowls with a few balls of meringue. Dust with a little grated nutmeg and accompany with langue de chats, if desired.

RICE PUDDING ARAGON STYLE

Serves 6

3 tbsp short-grain rice
pinch of salt
600ml / 1 pint milk
strip of lemon rind
pinch of cinnamon
9 tbsp sugar
3 eggs, separated

Place the rice in a saucepan with a pinch of salt. Cover with cold water, bring to the boil and cook for 5 minutes or until the water is absorbed. Add half the milk, stir to separate the grains of rice and allow the starch to go creamy. Add the remaining milk, the lemon rind, cinnamon and sugar. Cover and cook over low heat for 1¹/₂ hours, stirring from time to time to prevent sticking. Stir in the egg yolks. Beat the egg whites until stiff, add to the mixture and serve at once.

Left: Custard Pudding with Meringues
Right: Rice Pudding Aragon Style

MELON ICE-CREAM

Serves 4

1 small Cantaloupe melon
100g/4oz sugar
2 tbsp lemon juice
1 egg white

Decoration:
100ml/4fl oz double or whipping cream,
whipped
Maraschino cherries
crystallised angelica

Cut the melon into quarters. Remove and discard the seeds. Scoop out the flesh into a mixing bowl. Reform the shells into the original melon shape, wrap in aluminium foil and place in the freezer. Mash together the melon flesh with the sugar and lemon juice then beat with an electric whisk until the sugar has dissolved. Place in the freezer until half-frozen, then beat well again with an electric whisk.

Stiffly beat the egg white and fold into the melon mixture, blending them thoroughly. Pour into the frozen melon quarters. Wrap in aluminium foil and freeze for at least 4 hours. Remove the foil and separate the quarters, using a hot knife. Decorate each piece of melon with whipped cream and a cherry surrounded by chopped angelica.

AMERICAN MERINGUE

Serves 6

4 eggs, separated
250g/8oz sugar
butter, for greasing
1/4 litre/7 fl oz milk

Beat the egg whites with 100g/4 oz of the sugar until stiff. Place another 100g/4 oz of the sugar in a saucepan and heat until caramelised. Pour in a thin stream onto the egg whites, beating constantly.

Line a cake tin with greased aluminium foil. Turn the meringue mixture into the tin and cook in a bain-marie in the oven at 150°C/300°F/Gas Mark 2 for 1 1/2 hours or until a knife inserted in the centre comes out clean. Turn out onto a serving dish and leave to cool.

In a mixing bowl, beat the egg yolks with the remaining sugar. Heat the milk and stir in. Place the bowl over a pan of simmering water and cook, stirring, until creamy and thickened. Allow to cool, then use to cover the meringue.

CHOCOLATE TRIFLE

Serves 8-10

225g chocolate, chopped
75ml/3 fl oz strong black coffee
225g/8oz butter
75g/3oz sugar
40g/1 1/2 oz vanilla sugar
3 eggs, separated
100g/4oz ground almonds, toasted
300ml/1/2 pint double or whipping cream
24 sponge biscuits

Decoration:
75ml/3 fl oz double or whipping cream
25g/1oz flaked almonds

Coffee Sauce:
8 tbsp sugar
75ml/3 fl oz water
3 tbsp instant coffee granules
75ml/3 fl oz single cream

Grease a 1 1/4 litre/2 pint flan ring with butter, and line the base and sides with greased aluminium foil.

Melt the chopped chocolate with the coffee over a low heat.

Beat the butter and sugar together until creamy. Beating continuously, add the egg yolks one at a time. Still beating, add the melted chocolate which should be almost cold. Stir in the ground almonds, and finally beat the egg whites until stiff and stir in. Mix together carefully then stir in the whipped cream.

Stick the sponge fingers to the sides of the flan ring flush against one another – there must be no gaps through which the sauce might escape. Pour in the mixture and chill in the refrigerator for 4-5 hours or overnight.

Dip the mould in boiling water for a few seconds and turn out onto a serving dish. Garnish with the cream and flaked almonds.

Coffee Sauce: Place the sugar and water in a saucepan. Heat to dissolve the sugar then simmer for 4 minutes until syrupy. Remove from the heat, add the coffee and once it is dissolved, stir in the cream and reheat. Serve hot in a sauce boat or allow to cool and pour around the trifle.

HEAVENLY SWEETMEAT

Serves 6-8

1/2 kg/1lb sugar
100ml/4 fl oz water
12 egg yolks
2 egg whites
1 tsp grated lemon rind

Dissolve the sugar in the water then bring to the boil and cook for 5 minutes. Use enough of this syrup to coat a 26cm/10inch ring mould. Beat the egg yolks and whites together in a mixing bowl. Pour in the remaining syrup, add the lemon rind and stir well.

Pour the mixture into the mould. Cover the mould and cook in a bain-marie in the oven at 180°C/350°F/Gas Mark 4 for 20 minutes. Allow to cool in the water. Turn out and serve chilled.

Top: Heavenly Sweetmeat
Bottom: Chocolate Trifle

COFFEE SOUFFLÈ

Serves 4

3 eggs, separated
75g/3 oz sugar
2 tbsp instant coffee granules
150ml/¼ pint boiling water
15g/½ oz coffee or chocolate
3 tbsp cold water
200ml/7 fl oz double or whipping cream
2 tbsp rum

Praline:
50g/2oz flaked almonds
50g/2oz sugar

To make the praline, place the almonds in a non-stick cake tin. Dissolve the sugar in the water then boil until a deep caramel colour. Pour immediately over the nuts, then allow to cool and set. Remove from the tin, break into pieces and pulverise to a rough powder in a blender.

Great a 15cm/6 inch soufflé dish and wrap 2 layers of greaseproof paper around the outside allowing about 8cm/3 inches extra at the top. Grease the paper on the inside.

Place the egg yolks and sugar in a mixing bowl and beat until frothy. Dissolve the coffee in the boiling water. Add to the yolks, then place the bowl over a pan of simmering water and heat, stirring, until the mixture thickens. Remove from the heat, and continue beating while the mixture is cooling down. Place the jelly and cold water in a saucepan and dissolve the jelly over a low heat. Pour carefully into the soufflé dish. Leave to set in the refrigerator, lightly shaking the mould occasionally. Beat the cream until fairly stiff and carefully stir into the cold coffee mixture. Whisk the egg whites until they just hold their shape and fold into the mixture with the rum. Pour into the soufflé dish and chill for several hours. When the soufflé has set, carefully remove the paper, and coat the top in praline.

DEEP-FRIED CUSTARD CREAMS

Serves 6-8

1 tbsp cornflour
½ litre/¾ pint milk
strip of lemon rind
4 tbsp sugar

Top: Caramel Bavarois
Bottom: Deep-fried Custard Creams

pinch of salt
2 eggs
1 tbsp butter
75g/3oz fresh breadcrumbs
oil
cinnamon and sugar to finish

Dissolve the cornflour in a little of the milk. Bring the remaining milk to the boil in a small saucepan with the lemon rind, sugar and salt. Add the dissolved cornflour and stir until the mixture thickens. Remove from the heat. Add the yolk of one egg and the butter and stir well to combine. Pour into a serving dish and allow to cool. The mixture should come about 2.5cm/1 inch up the sides of the dish. Chill well then divide into small squares.

Beat together the remaining egg white and whole egg. Carefully remove the squares from the dish and coat with the egg and then the breadcrumbs. Deep-fry in very hot oil, and dry on kitchen paper to remove the excess grease. Roll in cinnamon powder mixed with sugar.

This dessert can also be served cold.

CARAMEL BAVAROIS

Serves 6

1½ litres/2½ pints milk
4 eggs, separated
15g/½ oz gelatine
300ml/½ pint double or whipping cream
8 tbsp sugar

Place the egg yolks in a mixing bowl and beat in half the sugar. Soak the gelatine in a little water. Place the remaining sugar in a saucepan with a little water and heat until dissolved. Simmer until a pale golden caramel then remove from the heat. Place the milk in a saucepan, bring to the boil and add the caramel and egg yolk mixture. Heat the gelatine and stir. Bring back to the boil, stirring continuously. Cool in a basin of water and ice-cubes, stirring from time-to-time.

Beat the egg whites until stiff and fold into the mixture when it is cold. The two mixtures must be at the same temperature otherwise they will not mix well and the two different colours will be visible in the dessert.

Wet a 22cm/8½ inch ring mould with cold water and pour in the mixture. Chill in the refrigerator for about 8 hours.

Dip the mould in boiling water and turn out onto a serving dish. To garnish, pipe whipped cream through a fluted nozzle. Serve with warm caramel sauce made as follows: heat together 50g/2oz sugar and a

squeeze of lemon juice. When the mixture is a pale golden colour, add 50ml/2 fl oz water and heat.

BANANAS FLAMBE

Serves 8

50g/2oz butter
8 bananas, peeled
6 dessertspoons sugar
juice of ½ lemon
juice of 4 oranges
3 dessertspoons Grand Marnier or sweet sherry
75ml/3 fl oz brandy

Melt the butter in a large frying pan. Add the bananas and cook for 8-10 minutes, turning carefully to avoid breaking them up.

Add the sugar and cook for 3 minutes until the sugar dissolves. Add the fruit juices and Grand Marnier or sherry and cook for 7-10 minutes until the sauce thickens.

Heat the brandy in a small saucepan. Pour onto the bananas and carefully light with a match. As soon as the flames die down, serve straight from the frying pan or on a heated serving dish.

FIGS WITH RASPBERRY SAUCE

Serves 4

24 dried figs
100ml/4 fl oz wine
100g/4oz sugar
250g/8oz raspberries

Place the figs in a saucepan with the wine, sugar and a little water and simmer until the liquid is reduced by half.

Meanwhile, liquidize the raspberries in a blender until smooth, then strain through a fine sieve to remove the seeds.

Pour the raspberry sauce onto individual serving plates. Pile the figs on top, and sprinkle over some cooking juices.

Opposite, top: Figs with Raspberry Sauce
Opposite, bottom: Rice Pudding with Heavenly Topping
Below: Chestnut Custard

CHESTNUT CUSTARD

Serves 6

500g/1lb chestnuts
175g/6oz sugar
1/2 litre/3/4 pint milk
1 cinnamon stick
4 eggs

With a sharp knife, score a cross on the side of each nut. Cook in boiling water until half-done. Drain and peel, then return to the water, adding enough milk to cover and 25g/1oz of the sugar. Continue cooking until tender then sieve to reduce to a purée. Place the milk and cinnamon stick in a saucepan and bring to the boil. Remove from the heat.

Place the eggs and 100g/4oz of the sugar in a mixing bowl and beat well together. Pour on the hot milk, mix well and add the chestnut purée.

Heat the remaining sugar until caramelised then use to coat the base of 6 individual ramekins. Pour in the chestnut custard, place in a roasting tin half-filled with hot water and cook in the oven at 170°C/325°F/Gas Mark 3 for 20-30 minutes. Allow to cool, then turn out onto serving dishes.

RICE PUDDING WITH HEAVENLY TOPPING

Serves 6

1/2 litre/3/4 pint milk
1 cinnamon stick
50g/2oz short-grain rice
100g/4oz sugar
Scant 15g/1/2 oz gelatine
100g/4oz preserved fruit or canned mixed fruit, drained

For the heavenly topping:
225g/8oz sugar
6 egg yolks, beaten

To make the topping, dissolve 50g/2oz of the sugar in a little water then boil until a golden syrup forms. Pour into a 600ml/1 pint soufflé dish. Dissolve the remaining sugar in water and cook until the syrup is fairly thick. Stir into the beaten egg yolks and pour onto the caramel in the dish. Steam or cook in a covered bain-marie for 30 minutes until the mixture sets. Remove the dish from the bain-maries.

To make the rice pudding, place the milk and cinnamon stick in a saucepan and bring to the boil. Add the rice and simmer for 20 minutes until tender. Add the sugar and cook, stirring, for 5 minutes. Remove from the heat.

Meanwhile, soak the gelatine in a little cold water and thinly slice the fruit. Heat the gelatine to dissolve and add to the rice mixture with the fruit. When the mixture is lukewarm pour into the soufflé dish. Chill well.

To serve, turn out onto a serving dish and decorate as you like.

COLD ORANGE AND LEMON SOUFFLE

Serves 4

15g/¹/₂ oz gelatine
4 eggs, separated
170g/6oz sugar
300ml/¹/₂ pint lemon juice
600ml/1 pint orange juice
2 tbsp Curacao, Cointreau or Grand Marnier
200ml/7 fl oz double or whipping cream

Decoration:
Whipped cream and grated orange rind

Grease a 15cm/6 inch soufflé dish and wrap 2 layers of greaseproof paper around the outside allowing about 8cm/3 inches extra at the top. Fasten with string.

Soak the gelatine in a little cold water. Place the egg yolks, sugar, lemon and orange juice in a mixing bowl and beat well. Place the bowl over a pan of simmering water and cook, stirring, until thickened. Heat the gelatine to dissolve and add to the egg mixture. Remove from the heat and allow to cook, stirring continuously. Stir in the liqueur. When cold, fold in the cream.

Beat the egg whites until stiff and carefully fold into the mixture. Pour into the dish and chill for several hours until the soufflé has set. Remove the greaseproof paper and decorate with whipped cream and grated orange rind.

VIENNESE PEARS

Serves 6

6 large pears, peeled
6 tbsp instant coffee granules
250g/8oz sugar
600ml/1 pint water
225ml/8fl oz cream

Place the pears in a flameproof casserole dish. Mix together the coffee granules, 50g/2oz of the sugar and the water and pour over the pears. Cover and simmer until the pears are tender. Remove the pears to a serving dish. Add the remaining sugar to the casserole dish and simmer until syrupy. Pour the coffee syrup over the pears and chill well.

CREPES SUZETTE

Makes 25

250g/8oz flour
Pinch of salt
3 eggs, beaten
600ml/1 pint milk
2 tbsp oil

For orange flambé sauce:
100g/4oz butter
grated rind and juice of 2 lemons
100g/4oz sugar
4 tbsp Curacao, Cointreau or Grand Marnier
4 tbsp brandy

Sift the flour and salt into a mixing bowl. Make a well in the centre, add the beaten eggs and gradually add half the milk, stirring constantly. Add the oil and beat until smooth. Add the remaining milk and leave to stand for 30 minutes.

Heat a knob of butter in a non-stick frying pan. Pour in 1 tablespoon batter and tilt the pan to spread the mixture. Cook until the underside is golden then turn over and cook the other side until golden. Stack the pancakes on a wire rack on top of each other. Keep covered with a tea towel. The pancakes can be made a day ahead.

To make the orange flambé sauce, melt the butter in a frying pan. Add the sugar, orange rind and juice and heat until bubbling. Dip each crêpe in the sauce, fold into quarters, then place on a warmed serving dish. Add the alcohol to the pan, heat gently, then ignite. Pour the flaming liquid over the crepes and serve immediately.

CHESTNUT CHARLOTTE

Serves 6-8

400g/14oz canned, sweetened chestnut purée
150g/5oz plain chocolate
2 tbsp milk
100g/4oz butter, softened
4 tbsp caster sugar
4 tbsp rum
¹/₄ litre/7 fl oz water
24 sponge fingers

Decoration:
150g/5oz plain chocolate
knob of butter
whipped cream

Place the chestnut purée in a mixing bowl. Melt the chocolate in the milk and add to the purée with the butter. Stir well to combine.

Grease a 1.1 litre/2 pint charlotte mould and line the sides with lightly greased, greaseproof paper.

Combine the sugar, rum and water. Dip the sponge fingers in this solution, lightly soaking most of them, but merely moistening a few. Stick the lightly soaked fingers against the sides of the mould. Pour in the chestnut mixture and cover with the moistened fingers.

Cut out a circle of greaseproof paper the same size as the top of the mould. Place on top of the charlotte, cover with a plate and weigh down. Chill overnight. Dip the mould in boiling water for a few seconds and turn out onto a serving dish.

Decorate with a chocolate sauce made from the chocolate and butter and pipe on whipped cream, if liked.

Top: Chestnut Charlotte
Bottom: Crêpes Suzette

FIRE AND ICE

Serves 4

4 Golden Delicious apples
4 tsp sugar
25g/1oz butter
75ml/3 fl oz cider
4 scoops vanilla ice-cream
4 walnut halves

Remove the core from the apples and score the skin all round horizontally. Place the apples in a baking dish and put a spoonful of sugar and a little ball of butter into each apple. Sprinkle with the cider. Bake in the oven at 190°C/375°F/Gas Mark 5 for 40-50 minutes.

While baking, the flesh of the apple will rise a little out of the circular cut; when they are done, remove the skin from this part of the apple. Mix the juice that is left in the ovenproof dish with some more cider or water and pour around the base of the apples. Place a scoop of ice-cream on each apple and top with a walnut half.

Opposite, top: Fire and Ice
Opposite, bottom: Sherry Bavarois
Below, left: Fig Meringue with
Walnut sauce
Below, right: Pears in Puff nPastry
with Pear Liqueur

SHERRY BAVAROIS

Serves 6-8

50g/2oz sultanas
150ml/1/4 pint sweet sherry
25g/1oz gelatine
6 eggs, separated
12 tbsp sugar

Decoration:
300ml/1/2 pint double or whipping cream, whipped

Sherry Sauce:
6 tbsp sugar
75ml/3 fl oz sherry

Soak the sultanas in a little of the sherry. Soak the gelatine in cold water. Place the egg yolks, half the sugar and the remaining sherry in a small mixing bowl. Whisk until the mixture is frothy then add the sultanas. Place the bowl over a pan of simmering water and cook, stirring, until the mixture thickens. Remove the bowl from heat, dissolve the gelatine and stir in. Cool in a basin filled with water and ice-cubes, stirring from time-to-time.

Beat the egg whites with the remaining sugar. When the sultana mixture is cold, carefully fold in the beaten egg whites. Grease a ring mould or loaf tin with oil and pour in the mixture. Chill for several hours.

Dip the mould in boiling water for a few seconds and turn out the bavarois onto a serving dish. Decorate with piped whipped cream and extra sultanas, if liked.

Serve with sherry sauce prepared as follows: Place the sugar in a saucepan with just enough water to cover. Stir over a low heat until the sugar dissolve. Increase the heat and simmer until it becomes a fairly thick syrup. Add the sherry. Can be served hot or cold.

PEARS IN PUFF PASTRY WITH PEAR LIQUEUR

Serves 1

1/2 large pear, peeled and sliced
1 oval puff pastry vol-au-vent
50g/2oz sugar
75ml/3 fl oz Poire William liqueur

Arrange the pear slices in the vol-au-vent shell. Bake in the oven at 190°C/375°F/Gas Mark 5 for 20 minutes until golden.

Place the sugar in a saucepan with just enough water to cover. Stir over a low heat until the sugar dissolves, increase the heat and simmer until light golden and syrupy. Add the liqueur, pour over the pear and serve hot, with an egg custard, if desired.

CHOCOLATE SOUFFLE

Serves 4

100g/4oz plain chocolate
1 tsp instant coffee granules
40g/1½ oz butter
40g/1½ oz flour
175ml/6 fl oz milk
50g/2oz sugar
few drops of vanilla essence
3 egg yolks
4 egg whites
Icing sugar

Topping:
150ml/¼ pint single cream
2 tbsp rum

Grease a 15cm/6 inch soufflé dish and wrap 2 layers of aluminium foil around the outside allowing about 8cm/3 inches extra at the top. Fasten with string and grease the foil inside.

Melt the chocolate with the coffee over a low heat or in the microwave.

Melt the butter in a saucepan, add the flour and stir to make a light roux. Stir in the milk at little at a time. Bring to the boil, stirring continuously. Stir in the sugar and vanilla essence and then the melted chocolate and coffee. Remove from heat and add the egg yolks one at a time, mixing well.

Beat the egg whites until stiff and mix into the chocolate mixture in 3 batches, taking care that the whites do not lose their volume. Pour the mixture into the mould. Make a groove about 2.5cm/1 inch deep with a teaspoon around the side of the soufflé mixture to help it rise.

Bake in the centre of the oven at 190°C/375°F/Gas Mark 5 for about 25 minutes. Remove the foil and serve immediately with the cream mixed with the rum.

FIG MERINGUE WITH WALNUT SAUCE

Serves 6

6 egg yolks
250g/8oz sugar
100g/4oz ready-made meringues, crumbled
½ litre/¾ pint double or whipping cream
150g/5oz fresh figs, peeled and chopped

For the walnut sauce:
½ litre/¾ pint milk
100g/4oz walnuts, chopped
100g/4oz sugar
pinch of cinnamon
50g/2oz white breadcrumbs

Place the egg yolks and sugar in a mixing bowl set over a pan of simmering water and beat together until spongy and thick. Remove from the heat and continue beating until cool. Add the broken meringue pieces, whipped cream and figs and freeze.

For the sauce, place the milk, walnuts, sugar and cinnamon in a saucepan. Bring to the boil, add the breadcrumbs and simmer for 30 minutes.

To serve, pour the sauce onto individual serving dishes and place spoonfuls of the frozen fig meringue on top.

RASPBERRIES WITH ALMOND BISCUITS

Serves 6

Raspberry Sauce:
200g/7oz raspberries
50g/2oz icing sugar

Almond Biscuits:
250g/8oz chopped almonds
250g/8oz sugar
25g/1oz flour
4 egg whites
Few drops of vanilla essence

Sieve the raspberries to make a purée and stir in the sugar.

For the biscuits, place the almonds, sugar, flour, egg whites and vanilla essence in a mixing bowl. Stir well until thoroughly blended. Drop spoonfuls of the mixture onto a greased baking sheet and bake in the oven at 180°C/350°F/Gas Mark 4 for 12-15 minutes until they harden.

To serve, flood individual serving dishes with the raspberry purée and place the almond biscuits on top. Decorate with extra raspberries and cream if desired.

CHOCOLATE MOUSSE SPONGE CAKE

Serves 4

Sponge Cake:
See Orange and Lemon "Punch" Cake (Page 56)

Mousse:
4 egg whites
200g/7oz plain chocolate
75g/3oz sugar
1/4 litre/7 fl oz double or whipping cream

Beat the egg whites with 25g/1oz of the sugar until the mixture will stand in stiff peaks. Melt the chocolate in a small mixing bowl placed over a pan of simmering water. Remove from the heat and allow to cool. When lukewarm, mix the chocolate into the meringue mixture. Beat the cream with the remaining sugar until slightly thickened, and add to the mixture. Line individual ramekins with slices of the sponge cake and pour in the mixture. Chill for several hours before serving, decorate to taste.

Top: Raspberries with Almond Biscuits
Bottom: Chocolate Mousse

STRAWBERRY BAVAROIS

Serves 6

1 x 170g/6oz can full cream evaporated milk
4 tbsp sugar
juice of ½ lemon
j15g/½ oz gelatine
1 jar strawberry jam

Decoration:
300ml/½ pint whipped cream and a few
strawberries

Chill the milk for 8 hours or overnight.
Soak the gelatine in a little cold water.

Whisk the milk with an electric mixer
until it is twice its original volume. Beat in
the lemon juice then carefully add the
sugar. Heat the gelatine to dissolve, add to
the mixture then carefully fold in the jam.

Wet a ring mould or individual
ramekins with cold water and pour in the
mixture. Chill until set. Dip in boiling
water for a few seconds and turn out onto
a serving dish. Décorate with piped
whipped cream.

This dish may be served with a strawberry sauce, made by puréeing fresh strawberries with icing sugar and a dash of
lemon juice.

CHESTNUT AND CHOCOLATE DESSERT

Serves 6

125g/4oz plain chocolate
2 dessertspoons milk
1½ kg/3lb canned chestnuts in syrup
75g/4oz butter, softened

Decoration:
80g/3½ oz plain chocolate, grated
2 egg whites

2 tbsp sugar

Place the chocolate and milk in a mixing
bowl set over a pan of simmering water
and heat until the chocolate melts. Set
aside.

Pour the syrup from the canned chestnuts into a mixing bowl and work in the
chocolate. Purée the chestnuts and stir in.
Add the softened butter and beat with a
whisk until the mixture is smooth. Grease
a 20cm/8 inch ring mould with butter and
pour in the mixture. chill overnight.

Dip the mould in boiling water for a
few seconds then turn out onto a serving
dish and dust with grated chocolate. Stiffly
whisk the egg whites and sugar together
and pipe the mixture into the centre and
around the outside of the dessert.
Alternatively use whipped cream.

CHOCOLATE AND ORANGE MOUSSE

Serves 8

200g/7oz plain chocolate
6 eggs, separated
6 tbsp sugar
150ml/¼ pint double or whipping cream
4 dessertspoons Cointreau
juice of 2 oranges
grated rind of 1 orange
2 gelatine leaves

Soak the gelatine in the orange juice and rind.

Melt the chocolate in a mixing bowl over a pan of simmering water. Add the butter, stirring until completely blended.

Heat the soaked gelatine until dissolved then pour onto the chocolate. Add the egg yolks one at a time and allow to cool.

Beat the egg whites with the sugar. When the chocolate mixture is cold, stir in the whipped cream, the liqueur and finally the egg whites.

Pour into a bowl and chill until serving.

Decorate with whipped cream and grated chocolate.

ALMOND APPLE WITH RASPBERRY SAUCE

Serves 1

1 large cooking apple, peeled and cored
25ml/1 fl oz custard sauce
50g/2oz ground almonds
250g/8oz raspberry sauce

Place a little sugar and butter inside the apple and a few drops of water. Bake in the oven at 180°C/350°F/gas mark 3 for 35-40 minutes until just tender. Fill with the almond sauce and serve in pool of raspberry sauce. Decorate to taste.

Almond Sauce:
Make a custard sauce (See recipe for Apple Tart with Blackberry Sauce on page 40) and add the ground almonds.

Raspberry Sauce:
(See Recipe for Raspberries with Almond Biscuits on Page 26)

Left: Chestnut and Chocolate Dessert
Right: Strawberry Bavarois

APPLE, APRICOT AND PRUNE TART

Serves 6

Sweet Pastry:
75g/3oz butter
150g/5oz flour
Pinch of salt
1 egg yolk
25g/1oz sugar
a little water

Filling:
250g/8oz apples, peeled and diced

Top: Almond Apple with Raspberry Sauce
Bottom: Apple, Apricot and Prune Tart

25g/2oz butter
75ml/3 fl oz rum
100g/2oz sugar
50g/2oz dried apricots, cooked
50g/2oz stoned prunes, cooked

Custard:
75g/3oz ground almonds
50g/2oz sugar
2 eggs
1/4 litre/7 fl oz single cream

Make the pastry: rub the butter into the sifted flour and salt. Stir in the egg yolk and sugar and enough water to bind to a dough. Knead lightly then chill for 30 minutes. Roll out the dough and use to line a flan tin.

To make the filling, soften the apples in the butter over a gentle heat. Flambe with the rum. Cook the sugar with a little water until caramelised, pour over the apples and simmer for 5 minutes.

For the custard, place all the ingredients in a heavy saucepan and cook over very low heat until thickened.

Fill the pastry shell with the caramelised apples and the cooked apricots and prunes. Pour over the custard and bake in the oven at 150°C/300°F/Gas Mark 2 for 1 1/2-2 hours.

CARROT CAKE

Serves 12

275g/10oz plain flour
1 level tsp bicarbonate of soda
2 level tsps baking powder
1 level tsp salt
175g/6oz soft light brown sugar
50g/2oz chopped walnuts
3 eggs
2 ripe bananas
175g/6oz grated carrots
175ml/6 fl oz oil

Frosting:
75g/3oz butter
75g/3oz cream cheese
175g/6oz icing sugar
1/2 tsp vanilla essence
finely chopped walnuts for sprinkling

Heat the oven to 180°C/350°F or gas mark 4. Grease and line a 9 inch (22.5cm) round cake tin. Sift the flour, bicarbonate of soda, baking powder and salt into a mixing bowl. Add the brown sugar, chopped walnuts and eggs. Peel and mash the bananas and add to the bowl, then add the grated carrots and oil. Mix ingredients together, then beat well for 1 minute to make a soft cake batter.

Pour mixture into prepared cake tin and spread level. Place in centre of oven and bake for 1 hour. Allow to cool in tin for 5 minutes, then turn out onto a wire rack and leave until completely cool.

Put the butter and cream cheese into a mixing bowl, sift in the icing sugar, add the vanilla and beat until soft and creamy. Slice cake horizontally and sandwich layers with a little of the frosting. Spread remainder over top and sides, then sprinkle with finely chopped walnuts.

CAKES AND FLANS

SANTIAGO ALMOND CAKE

Serves 6

Pastry:
3 tbsp oil
3 tbsp milk
50ml/2 fl oz water
250g/8oz flour
Pinch of salt
1 tbsp sugar

Filling:
4 eggs
200g/7oz sugar
grated rind of 1 lemon
pinch of cinnamon
200g/7oz ground almonds
icing sugar

Place the oil, milk and water in a mixing bowl and whisk together with a fork. Gradually sift in the flour and salt, mixing with a knife. Add the sugar. Knead lightly and chill for 30 minutes. Roll out thinly and use to line a flan tin.

Beat together the eggs, sugar, lemon rind and cinnamon until fluffy. Add the almonds with a spatula, a little at a time. Pour into the pastry shell and bake in the oven at 180°C/350°F/Gas Mark 4 for 45–50 minutes until golden brown.

Cut out a decorative shape in paper and place in the centre of the cake. Dust in icing sugar and remove the paper.

MARIFE CAKE

Serves 6-8

125g/4oz butter
75g/3oz granulated sugar
3 eggs, separated
200g/7oz flour
1 tsp baking powder
200g/7oz caster sugar
Grated rind of 1 lemon
250g/8oz ground almonds
1 jar (340g/12oz) apricot jam

Place the butter and granulated sugar in a mixing bowl and beat together. Stir in the egg yolks one at a time, then add the flour and baking powder. Grease a

30cm/12inch cake tin with and dust with flour. Line the base and sides of a loose-based tin with little balls of the dough, pressing down well so they stick together.

Beat the egg whites until stiff. Add the caster sugar, lemon rind and finally the ground almonds. Cover the bottom of the pastry shell with apricot jam and pour over the almond meringue, spreading it out with a spatula.

Bake in the oven at 180°C/350°F/Gas Mark 4 for 1 hour. If after 30 minutes the top is browned, cover with greased aluminium foil.

LIGHT SPONGE CAKE

Serves 6-8

3 eggs, separated
5 heaped tbsp sugar
4 1/2 tbsp flour
6 1/2 tbsp cornflour
1/2 tsp baking powder
1 tsp salt

Place the egg yolks and sugar in a mixing bowl and beat until light and frothy. (This should take about 3 minutes with an electric whisk or 7 minutes by hand.)

Santiago Almond Cake

Beat the egg whites until stiff and fold into the egg yolk mixture. Sift the flour, corn-flour, baking powder and salt into the mixture. Mix gently, taking care not to flatten the mixture. Pour into a greased and floured 24cm/9inch cake tin.

Bake in the oven at 180°C/325°F/Gas Mark 3 for 30 minutes. Turn out onto a wire rack while still warm and leave to cool.

STRAWBERRY AND CREAM SPONGE CAKE

Serves 6

3 egg whites
pinch of salt
3 tbsp sugar
2 egg yolks
3 tbsp flour
1 tsp baking powder
knob of butter

Syrup:
1/4 litre /7 fl oz water
125g/4oz sugar
75ml/3 fl oz rum

Place the egg whites in a mixing bowl with the salt and beat until stiff. Add the sugar, egg yolks and gradually incorporate the flour sifted with the baking powder.

Grease a ring mould with butter. Pour in the mixture and bake in the oven at 180°C/250°F/Gas Mark 4 for about 30 minutes.

Meanwhile, prepare the syrup. Place all the ingredients in a saucepan and heat gently to dissolve the sugar, then simmer for about 5 minutes until syrupy. Pour the hot syrup over the cooked sponge while it is still in the ring mould. Leave to cool then turn out and decorate with strawber-ries and whipped cream.

FRUIT PUDDING

Serves 6

1/2 kg/1lb pears, peeled and sliced
1/2 kg/1lb apples, peeled and sliced
Grated rind and juice of 1 lemon
Grated rind of 1 orange
4 tbsp chopped walnuts
4 tbsp sugar
100g/4oz butter
100g/4oz sugar
2 eggs
100g/4oz flour
1 tsp baking powder
3 tsp milk

Arrange the fruit in the base of a ring mould or baking dish. Sprinkle over the lemon juice, grated lemon and orange rind, walnuts and the 4 tablespoons of sugar. Bake in the oven at 180°C/350°F/gas mark 4 for 20 minutes until the fruit is soft.

Place the butter and remaining sugar in a mixing bowl and beat well together, then beat in the remaining ingredients. Pour over the fruit and return to the oven for about 40 minutes until golden brown.

BAKED APPLE PUDDING

Serves 6

3 eggs
the equivalent weight of butter, sugar and flour
1 tsp baking powder
3 apples, peeled and thinly sliced

Beat the eggs and sugar with an electric whisk until frothy. Add the butter, which should be soft, then add the flour mixed with the baking powder.

Grease a ring mould with butter, sprin-kle with flour and pour in the mixture. Top with a layer of the sliced apples. Dust with sugar and bake in the oven at 180°C/350°F/Gas Mark 4 for 1 hour. If the top is browning too quickly, cover with greased aluminium foil.

Turn out onto a plate and then over onto a serving dish so that the apples are on top. Dust with icing sugar and serve.

CARIBBEAN PINEAPPLE CAKE

Serves 8

50g/2oz granulated sugar
50ml/2 fl oz water
1 large can pineapple rings
4 eggs
125g/4oz caster sugar
125g/4oz flour
1 tsp baking powder
50ml/2 fl oz whisky

Dissolve the granulated sugar in the water then simmer until it is a light golden, caramel colour. Pour into a shallow cake tin and tilt to coat the base and sides. Leave to cool. Drain the pineapple rings and reserve the juice. Arrange the rings on the caramel.

Beat together the eggs and sugar and gradually stir in the flour and baking pow-der. Pour the mixture into the tin and bake in the oven at 180°C/350°F/gas mark 4 for 20-25 minutes or until a

skewer inserted in the centre comes out clean. Remove from the oven, sprinkle over the whisky and enough reserved pineapple juice to moisten the cake. Leave to cool then turn out onto a serving dish and decorate the sides with whipped cream, if liked.

Top: Fruit Pudding
Bottom: Baked Apple Pudding

GERMAN BLACKBERRY TART

Serves 6

3 cloves
Pinch of salt
1 tsp cinnamon
pinch each of black pepper, powdered bay
leaves, nutmeg and cumin seeds
1 tsp aniseed
1 hard-boiled egg, chopped
100g/4oz sugar
grated rind of 1 lemon and 1 orange
150g/5oz butter
1 egg, beaten
100g/4oz flour
1 jar blackberry jam

Pound together all the spices, chopped hard-boiled egg, sugar and grated fruit rinds.

Cream together the butter and beaten egg and stir in the spice mixture. Gradually add the flour to make a dough and knead lightly. Chill for 30 minutes then divide the pastry dough into 2 pieces, one 3 times the size of the other. Roll out the larger piece of pastry and use to line the base and sides of a greased shallow spring-clip tin. Fill the pastry with the jam. Roll out the smaller piece of dough, cut into strips and lay in a lattice pattern over the jam. Bake in the oven at 180°C/350°F/gas mark 4 for 30-35 minutes.

GERMAN CAKE

Serves 6

125g/4oz butter
75g/3oz granulated sugar
3 eggs, separated
200g/7oz flour
1 tsp baking powder
250g/8oz caster sugar
250g/8oz ground almonds
grated rind of 1 lemon
1 jar apricot jam

Place the butter and granulated sugar in a mixing bowl and beat together. Gradually add the egg yolks then sift in the flour with the baking powder, mixing well. Grease and flour a baking tin with detach-able sides and line the base with the dough.

Place the egg whites in a mixing bowl and beat until stiff. Gradually beat in the caster sugar, ground almonds and grated lemon rind. Spread the apricot jam over the dough, pour over the egg and almond mixture and bake in the oven at

180°C/350°F/gas mark 4 for 30 minutes.
Serve dusted with icing sugar, if desired.

FRUIT TART

Serves 6-8

Pastry:
200g/7oz flour
pinch of salt
150g/5oz butter
1 egg yolk
2 tsp sugar
4-5 tsp water

Fruit:
2 large mandarin oranges, peeled and segmented
2-3 pineapple rings, halved
2-3 peach halves or kiwi fruit, sliced
8-9 morello cherries, chopped

Apricot glaze:
1 jar apricot jam
juice of 1 lemon

Sift the flour and salt into a mixing bowl and rub in the butter. Beat the egg yolk, sugar and half the water together and use to bind the mixture to a dough, adding more water as necessary. Knead lightly and chill for 30 minutes.

Roll out the pastry to 1 cm/½ inch thickness and use to line a flan tin. Line the pastry case with aluminium foil, fill with dried beans and bake in the oven at 200°C/400°F/gas mark 6 for 30 minutes, removing the foil and beans after 15 min-utes. Leave to cool.

To make the glaze, cook the apricot jam with the lemon juice for 5 minutes, then pass through a sieve. Lay out the fruit in patterns in the pastry case and pour over the apricot glaze. Leave to cool.

PINEAPPLE UPSIDE-DOWN CAKE

Serves 8

75g/3oz butter
100g/4oz muscovado sugar
6 canned pineapple rings
a few morello cherries in syrup
4 eggs
170g/6oz granulated sugar
4 tbsp pineapple juice from tin
170g/6oz flour
1 tbsp baking powder

Melt the butter and muscovado sugar together then pour into a 23 cm/9 inch cake tin. Lay a pattern of pineapple rings and morello cherries on top.

Above: Fruit Tart
Right: German Cake

Beat the eggs with the granulated sugar until frothy. Add the pineapple juice, and mix well. Carefully whisk in the flour and baking powder. Pour the mixture into the cake tin, and bake in the oven at 180°C/350°F/Gas Mark 4 for 50-60 min-utes until the sponge springs back when lightly pressed.

Turn out onto a serving dish and eat while still warm.

GENOESE SPONGE

Serves 6

4 eggs
2 egg yolks
150g/5oz sugar
150g/5oz flour
1 tsp baking powder
60g/2 ¹/₂ oz butter, melted and cooled

Place the eggs, egg yolks and sugar in a bowl over a pan of simmering water. Whisk for 5-10 minutes until light and thick. Remove the bowl from the heat and continue whisking for 5 minutes. Sift in the flour and baking powder and carefully fold in with the melted butter.

Grease a cake tin with butter, line it with greaseproof paper and grease the paper with butter as well. Pour in the cake mixture and bake in the oven at 180°C/350°F/gas mark 4 for about 25 minutes.

CHOCOLATE AND WALNUT CAKE

Serves 6-8

100g/4oz butter
100g/4oz sugar
3 eggs, separated
100g/4oz plain chocolate
25g/5oz flour
150g/5oz ground walnuts

Filling:
300ml/¹/₂ pint whipping cream

Topping:
100ml/3fl oz single cream
100g/4oz plain chocolate, chopped

Place the butter and sugar in a mixing bowl and beat until smooth. Beat in the egg yolks on at a time. Melt the chocolate and stir into the butter mixture. Combine the flour with the ground walnuts and blend into the mixture with a spatula. Finally, beat the egg whites stiffly and fold into the mixture with a circular motion.

Grease and flour an 18cm/7 inch spring-clip cake tin. Pour in the mixture and bake for about 55 minutes in the oven at 180°C/350°F/Gas Mark 4. The cake is done when a knife which has been inserted knife comes out clean. Turn out onto a wire rack and leave to cool.

Cut the sponge in half. Place one half on a serving dish and pipe on the whipped cream. Place the other half on top.

Topping: Heat the single cream in a heavy-based saucepan or bain-marie. Add the chopped chocolate and stir until completely dissolved. Remove from heat and allow to cool, stirring constantly. When the mixture is quite thick, pour over the cake and leave to set.

Below: Genoese Sponge
Opposite, top: Chocolate and Walnut Cake
Opposite, bottom: Chestnut Cake

CHESTNUT CAKE

Serves 6-8

1/2 kg/1lb chestnuts
150g/5oz plain chocolate
150g/5oz butter
150g/5oz icing sugar

Score a cross on the side of each nut. Boil for a few minutes, then drain and peel off the shell and inner skin. Simmer in boiling salted water for 30-40 minutes until tender, then drain and sieve to a purée.

Melt the chocolate in a saucepan, add the butter and icing sugar and beat until creamy. Add the chestnut purée.

Grease a ring mould and line with aluminium foil. Pour in the mixture and chill in the refrigerator. Turn out and decorate with whipped cream.

AUTUMN FRUIT TART

Serves 6-8

200g/7oz butter
75g/3oz icing sugar
4 egg whites
1 tsp vanilla essence
200g/7oz flour
1 tsp black coffee
Choice of prepared fruit:
Kiwi fruit
Bananas
Pears
Apples
Strawberries
Oranges

To make the pastry, beat the butter with the icing sugar until smooth. Add the egg whites one at a time, with the coffee and vanilla essence, then sift over the flour and carefully fold in. Leave to stand for 30 minutes.

Roll out and use to line a cake tin. Bake blind in the oven for 20 minutes. Remove and pile on top slices and segments of your chosen fruits, alternating the different colours. Dust with a little sugar before baking in the oven at 180°C/250°F/Gas Mark 4 for 40 minutes. Serve hot.

APRICOT TART

Serves 6-8

Pastry:
200g/7oz flour
1/2 tsp salt
100g/4oz butter
1 tbsp sugar

Filling:
3 egg yolks
150g/5oz sugar
50g/2oz butter, softened
100g/4oz ground almonds
75ml/3fl oz rum
1 kg/2.2 lbs apricots, halved and stoned

Decoration:
3 tbsp apricot jam
75ml/3fl oz rum
25g/1oz almonds, chopped

Sift the flour and salt into a mixing bowl. Rub in the butter then stir in the sugar. Add enough water to bind to a firm dough. Knead lightly, then leave to stand for 30 minutes.

Beat the egg yolks and sugar together until frothy. Add the softened butter, ground almonds and rum.

Roll out the pastry and line a 26cm/10inch greased flan tin. Pour the almond mixture into the pastry shell and place the apricot halves close together on top.

Bake in the oven at 220°C/425°F/gas mark 7 for 35 minutes. Heat the apricot jam and rum together, brush over the top of the tart and sprinkle over the chopped almonds. Bake for 5 more minutes in a hot oven or under the grill to brown the top.

AMERICAN-STYLE APPLE PIE

Serves 6

1 kg/2.2 lbs apples, peeled and sliced
100ml/4fl oz water
juice of 1 lemon
1 tsp cinnamon
300g/10oz flour
150g/5oz butter
2 eggs, separated
100g/4oz sugar
pinch of salt

Place the apples in a saucepan with the water, lemon juice and cinnamon, cover and simmer for 10 minutes.

To make the pastry, place the flour, butter, egg yolks, sugar and salt in a food processor and process for a few seconds to form a dough. Alternatively, place the flour on a board, make a well in the centre and gradually incorporate the remaining pastry ingredients, using the fingertips. Knead well and chill for 30 minutes.

Grease a 22cm/8 1/2 inch flan tin. Roll out the dough very thinly and line the tin leaving about 2.5cm/1 inch hanging over the sides and base. Prick with a fork, to prevent it rising, and pour in the apple mixture.

Make a ball with the leftover dough, roll out and cut into strips and arrange in a lattice on top of the tart. Fold the dough at the sides over the lattice. Brush the top with lightly beat egg white and bake in the oven at 190°C/275°F/gas mark 5 for about 25 minutes.

Apricot tart

APPLE TART WITH BLACKBERRY SAUCE

Serves 6

Pastry:
250g/8oz flour
50g/2oz butter
1 egg yolk
a little water
pinch of salt

Filling:
50g/2oz raisins, soaked in sweet wine
3 apples, peeled and finely sliced

100g/4oz apricot jam

Custard Sauce:
25g/1oz flour
2 egg yolks
75g/3oz sugar
¼ litre/7fl oz milk
few pinches of cinnamon

Blackberry Sauce:
350g/12oz blackberries, sieved
25g/1oz icing sugar

Make the pastry as for American-style

Apple Pie (Pg 38), substituting the water for the sugar. roll out and line a 22cm/8 inch greased flan tin. Pinch the base.

To make the custard sauce and filling, place the flour, egg yolks and sugar in a heavy-based saucepan. Heat the milk and cinnamon in another pan until boiling, then pour over the flour mixture. Cook, whisking constantly, until thickened. Remove from the heat and add the raisins. Allow to cool slightly then pour into the pastry case. Arrange the apple slices on top and bake in the oven at 180°C/350°F/Gas Mark 4 for 45 minutes. Glaze with warmed apricot jam, if liked, and serve with a sauce made from the sieved black-berries.

Above: Pineapple in Rum Sauce
Opposite: Apple Tart with Blackberry Sauce

PINEAPPLE IN RUM SAUCE

Serves 6

6 pineapple rings

Rum Sauce:
1/2 litre/3/4 pint milk
4 egg yolks
125g/4oz sugar
15g/1/2 oz cornflour
75ml/3fl oz rum

Place the egg yolks, sugar, cornflour and
rum in a saucepan and whisk until smooth.
   Bring the milk to boil, allow to cool
until lukewarm and pour over the egg
mixture. Stir well, bring back to the boil,
stirring continuously, and simmer until
thickened. Remove from the heat and
leave to cool.
   Arrange the pineapple slices on serving
plates and pour around the rum sauce.
Decorate to taste.

BASQUE CAKE

Serves 10

250g/8oz butter
3 eggs
200g/7oz sugar
100g/4oz ground almonds
250g/8oz flour

Sauce:
50g/2oz raisins
50ml/2 fl oz rum
1/2 litre/3/4 pint milk
3 egg yolks
125g/4oz sugar
1 tbsp cornflour

Beat the butter until soft. Beat the eggs and sugar with an electric mixer until very pale, then add to the butter, beating well. Mix the almonds with the flour, sprinkle onto the egg mixture and carefully fold in.

To make the sauce, soak the raisins in the rum. Bring the milk to the boil. Beat the eggs, sugar and cornflour in a heavy-based saucepan. Pour on the boiling milk, stirring continuously over the heat until the mixture thickens.

Grease and flour a 30cm/12 inch spring-clip flan tin. Add the rum to the almond mixture, and pour half into the tin. Mix the raisins with the sauce and pour onto the almond mixture. Cover with the remaining almond mixture and bake in the oven at 180°C/350°F/Gas Mark 4 for 1 hour. Check the cake occasionally while cooking. If the edges rise too fast, increase the temperature; if the centre rises quickly, decrease the temperature. If the cake browns too quickly, cover with grease-proof paper.

BRIOCHE

Makes 1kg/2.2lbs dough

2 tbsp warm milk
15g/1/2 oz fresh yeast
2 tbsp sugar
500g/1lb strong plain white flour
15g/1/2 oz salt
125g/4oz butter
4 eggs, beaten

Place the milk, yeast and sugar in a mixing bowl and mix well. Add one-quarter of the flour and leave to stand in a warm place for 20 minutes until frothy. Place the remaining flour and the salt in a mixing bowl and rub in the butter until the mixture resembles breadcrumbs. Add the beaten eggs and mix well until the dough leaves the side of the bowl clean. Knead well then leave to rise until doubled in size; 1½ hours at room temperature, 4 hours in a cool place or up to 12 hours in the refrigerator.

Knead again on a lightly floured board for about 2 minutes. Use as directed (see recipe for Parisian Brioche on page 44).

APPLE STRUDEL

Serves 6-8

100g/4oz currants
75ml/3fl oz sweet sherry
1kg/2.2lb apples, peeled and sliced
350g/12oz sugar
strip of lemon rind
100ml/4fl oz water
450g/1lb flour
300g/10oz butter
1 egg, beaten

Soak the currants in the sherry.

Place the apples in a saucepan with 5 tbsp of the sugar, the lemon rind, currants and water. Simmer, uncovered, until the liquid has evaporated.

Place the flour in a mixing bowl. Rub in the butter and stir in the remaining sugar. Add enough water to bind to a dough. Knead lightly, then roll out the dough to a length of about 30cm/12 inches. Place the

Basque Cake

apples down the centre and fold over and seal the edges. Turn over and decorate the top with lattice strips made from the pastry trimmings. Brush with beaten egg and bake in the oven at 180°C/350°F/gas mark 4 for 25-30 minutes.

CHOCOLATE CHEESECAKE

Serves 8

200g/7oz digestive biscuits
75g/3oz butter, melted
2 tbsp sweet sherry

Apple Strudel

1/2kg/1lb cream cheese
150g/5oz butter
150g/5oz sugar
15g/1/2 oz gelatine
juice of 1 lemon
75g/3oz plain chocolate, melted
150g/5oz milk chocolate, melted

Crush the biscuits with a rolling pin or in a blender. Mix in the melted butter and the sherry. Press into the base of a 20cm/8 inch cake tin. Bake for 10 minutes in the oven at 180°C/350°F/gas mark 4.

Beat together the cheese, butter and sugar. Soak the gelatine in the lemon juice, heat until dissolved then add to the cheese mixture. Divide the mixture in two, and add the melted plain chocolate to one half.

When the cheesecake base is cold, pour on the chocolate mixture and chill for a few minutes in the refrigerator to firm up. Pour the remaining cheese mixture on top, and chill until set.

Pour the melted milk chocolate onto the cheesecake before removing the tin. Make a few patterns in the chocolate with a fork and allow to set.

LEMON CHEESECAKE

Serves 6

200g/7oz Nice biscuits
100g/4oz butter, melted
100g/4oz sugar
2 tbsp lemon juice
grated rind of 1 lemon

Filling:
1/2kg/1lb cream cheese or Philadelphia cheese
4 eggs, separated
grated rind of 3 lemons
200g/7oz sugar
200ml/7f oz double or whipping cream
25g/1oz gelatine
Juice of 1 lemon

Decoration:
Raspberries
Blackberries
Strawberries
Glacé fruits

Crush the biscuits with a rolling pin or in a blender. Mix in the melted butter, sugar, lemon juice and rind. Grease a 26cm/10 inch tin with detachable sides, press the mixture into the base and bake for 15 minutes in the oven at 180°C/350°F/gas mark 4. Allow to cool. Meanwhile, beat the cheese, egg yolks, lemon rind and half the sugar together until thoroughly mixed. Add the whipped cream.

Soak the gelatine in the lemon juice. Heat to dissolve then blend with the cheese mixture. Chill in the refrigerator for several minutes until the mixture has firmed up. Stiffly beat the egg whites with the remaining sugar and fold into the cheesecake mixture with the lemon rind. Pour onto the base, smooth the surface and chill for 3-4 hours.

To turn out, pass a hot knife around the sides and place the cheesecake on a serving dish. Decorate with fruits to taste and serve with cream, if desired.

RUSSIAN CAKE

Serves 8

Almond slices:
4 egg whites
4 tbsp sugar
4 tbsp ground almonds
4 tbsp cornflour
1 tsp baking powder

Filling:
1/2 litre/3/4 pint milk
Grated rind of 1 lemon
3 egg yolks

8 tbsp sugar
3 tbsp cornflour
100g/4oz butter
Icing sugar for dusting

To make the almond slices, stiffly beat the egg whites with the sugar. Mix together the almonds, cornflour and baking powder and carefully fold into the beaten egg whites to make a dough.

Cover a 25cm x 3cm /10 inch x 14 inch baking tray with greased greaseproof paper and sprinkle with flour. Roll out the almond dough as evenly as possible and trim to a square or oblong shape. Place on the baking tray and bake in the oven at 170°C/325°F/Gas Mark 3 for 20-25 minutes.

Meanwhile, make the filling. Bring the milk and lemon rind to boil. Beat in the egg yolks, sugar and cornflour and cook until the mixture thickens. Add the butter a little at a time and remove from the heat. Leave to cool completely. It should have a spreading consistency.

Remove the almond meringue from the oven and cut in half horizontally. Leave to cool. Place one half on a serving dish and spread over the filling. Cover with the second meringue half and dust with icing sugar.

PARISIAN BRIOCHE

Serves 10

350g/12 oz brioche dough (see page 42)
Butter and flour
1 egg, beaten with 1 tsp water

Turn out the dough onto a lightly floured work surface. Tear off about 75g/3oz for the crown of the loaf.

Roll the rest of the dough into a ball, and place in a greased, floured 20cm/8 inch tin. Make a hole in the top of the ball. Make a pear-shaped ball with the smaller piece of dough and place on top of the first ball, with the narrow end of the pear in the hole.

Cover and leave at room temperature for 1½ hours. Brush with the beaten egg and water mixture and bake in the oven at 200°C/400°F/gas mark 6 for about 35 minutes. Turn out while still warm.

This method may be used to make individual brioche loaves.

LEMON PIE

Serves 6-8

Pastry:
100g/4oz butter
50g/2oz sugar
200g/7oz flour

Filling:
4 eggs
300g/10oz sugar
4 lemons
60g/2½ oz butter

Topping:
4 egg whites
4 tbsp sugar

Place the butter and sugar in a mixing bowl and beat until creamy. Gradually incorporate the flour. Press the dough into a greased and floured loose-bottomed flan tin. Bake blind in the oven at 180°C/350°F/Gas Mark 4 for 25 minutes.

To make the filling, beat the eggs and sugar in a small mixing bowl. Add the lemon juice and place over a pan of simmering water. Add the butter, a little at a time, and cook until creamy and thickened. Pour into the pastry case.

Stiffly beat the egg whites and sugar, pile on top of the filling and return to the oven for few minutes until lightly browned.

Top: Russian Cake
Bottom: Lemon Cheesecake

CARAMEL TOPPED CAKE

Serves 6

4 eggs
125g/4oz sugar
125g/4oz flour

Filling:
5 egg yolks
1 heaped tbsp cornflour
225g/8oz sugar
300ml/½ pint milk

Mix the eggs and sugar in a mixing bowl
and fold in the sifted flour.

Pour into a greased and floured cake tin
and bake in the oven at 180°C/350°F/gas
mark 4 for 40 minutes.

Place the egg yolks, cornflour and
150g/5oz of the sugar in a heavy based
saucepan or bain-marie. Mix thoroughly,
add the milk and cook for 10 minutes,
stirring constantly over a gentle heat.

Cut the sponge in half horizontally and
spread over the cooled filling. Replace the
top half.

Place the remaining sugar in a saucepan
with 3 tbsp water, dissolve the sugar over a
low heat. Increase the heat and simmer
until a golden caramel then pour immediately over the cake. Allow to cool and
decorate the sides with almonds and
whipped cream, if desired.

WALNUT CHEESECAKE

Serves 6-8

200g/7oz digestive biscuits
100g/4oz butter, melted
50g/2oz sugar
2 tbsp sweet sherry or brandy

Filling:
½ kg/1lb cream cheese
8 tbsp clear honey
5 eggs, separated
100ml/4fl oz single cream
60g/2½ oz flour
100g/4oz sugar
150g/5oz walnuts, chopped

Decoration:
Walnut halves
Icing sugar

Crush the biscuits to a fine powder with a
rolling pin. Place in a mixing bowl and stir
in the melted butter, sugar and sherry or
brandy. Press the mixture into a 26cm/10
inch greased, loose-bottomed tin and set
aside.

To make the filling, place the cheese,

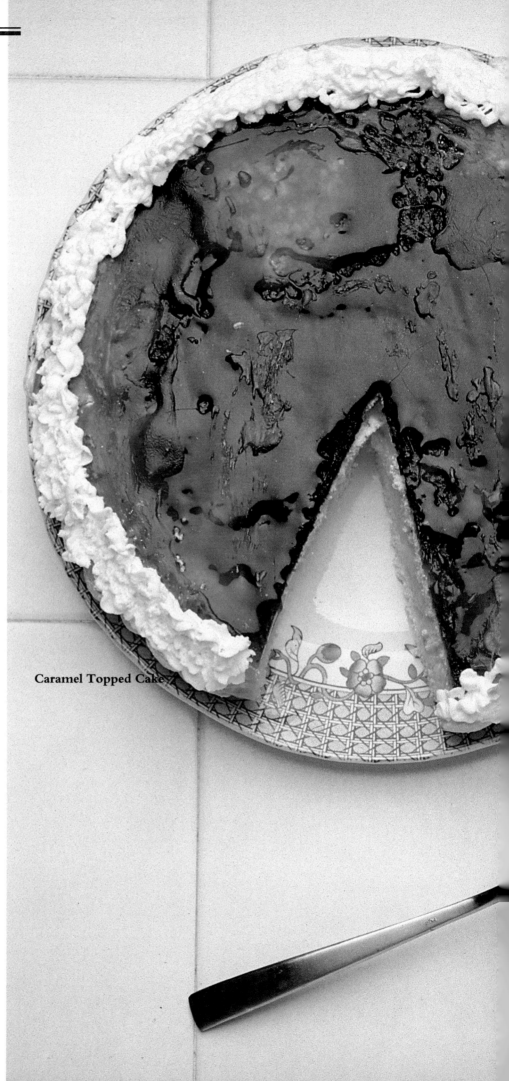

Caramel Topped Cake

honey, egg yolks, cream and flour in a mixing bowl and beat well. Stiffly beat the egg whites and sugar. Fold carefully into the cheese mixture and add the chopped walnuts. Pour onto the biscuit base and smooth the top.

Bake in the oven at 180°C/350°F/Gas Mark 4 for 50-60 minutes. If the edges rise faster than the centre during cooking time, increase the heat slightly. If the centre rises quickly, decrease the hat. Leave to cool in the oven with the door open, for 1 hour. Remove from the tin, decorate with walnut halves and dust with icing sugar.

MANDARIN CHOCOLATE SPONGE

Serves 4

4 mandarin oranges, peeled and segmented
175ml/7fl oz Cointreau
200g/7oz light sponge cake (see page 32)
200g/7oz milk chocolate
1 kiwi fruit, peeled and sliced

Strawberry Sauce:
250g/8oz strawberries, sieved
200g/7oz sugar

Marinate the mandarin orange segments in the Cointreau.

To make the strawberry sauce, mix the sieved strawberries with the icing sugar and pour onto a serving dish.

Place the sponge cake in the centre. Melt the chocolate in a mixing bowl placed over a pan of simmering water and pour over the cake. Decorate with the marinated mandarin segments and sliced kiwi fruit.

**Top: Mandarin Chocolate Sponge
Bottom: Light Sponge Cake (see page 31)**

PASTRIES, BISCUITS AND SWEETS

SUGAR SWEETS

Makes 24

200g/7 oz sugar
75ml/3fl oz water
12 egg yolks
Sugar for coating

Place the sugar and water in a saucepan, dissolve over a low heat, then increase the heat and simmer until a syrup forms. The syrup is ready when small amounts dropped into cold water will form soft balls.

Place the egg yolks in a heavy-based saucepan. Pour on the syrup a little at a time and cook over a low heat, stirring until the syrup and yolks are thoroughly mixed and the mixture no longer sticks to the sides of the saucepan.

Pour the mixture onto a marble top, if available, to cool it quickly, and roll out thinly. Once it is cold, form into a ball. Clean the surface and dust with icing sugar.

Roll the ball into a thick stick and cut into pieces the size of small eggs. Form each piece into a ball, roll in sugar and place into paper cases.

COCONUT BALLS

Makes 24

250g/8oz grated fresh coconut
250g/8oz sugar
75ml/3fl oz water
dessicated coconut for coating

Place the sugar and water in a saucepan, dissolve over a low heat then increase the heat and simmer until syrupy. The syrup is ready when small amounts dropped into cold water will form stiff threads.

Add the coconut and stir well. While the mixture is still hot, form into balls the size of small eggs, roll them in dessicated coconut and place into paper cases.

STRAWBERRY MERINGUE NESTS

Makes 20

125g/4oz icing sugar

2 egg whites
200ml/7fl oz double or whipping cream
225g/8oz strawberries

Place the icing sugar and egg whites in a mixing bowl over a pan of simmering water. Using an electric whisk, beat until the mixture is shiny and stiff. Remove the bowl from the heat and continue beating until the mixture has cooled.

Spoon the meringue into a forcing bag with a small fluted nozzle. Grease a baking tray, and cover with greaseproof paper.

Top: Sugar Sweets and Coconut Balls

Pipe the meringue onto the tray in little nest shapes about 4cm/1 ½ inches in diameter. Start with piping a solid base then add 2 rings on top of that.

Bake in the oven at 150°C/300°F/gas mark 2 for 1½-2 hours until the meringue is dry, but not golden. Remove the paper while still hot, and allow to cool.

Place the nests on a serving dish and pipe them full of whipped cream. Make little hollows in the middle of the nests, and put a strawberry in each hollow.

The nests by themselves will keep for 3 weeks if stored in an airtight tin. Once the cream is added they must be consumed the same day.

LEMON TARTS

Makes 24

200g/7oz flour
pinch of salt
100g/4oz butter
1 egg yolk
2 tbsp sugar
4 tbsp water

Filling:
2 eggs
8 tbsp sugar
grated rind and juice of 2 lemons
50g/2oz butter

Decoration:
¼ litre/7fl oz double or whipping cream

To make the pastry, sift the flour and salt into a mixing bowl. Rub in the butter then add the remaining ingredients and mix to a dough. Knead lightly and chill for 30 minutes. Roll out the pastry to ½ cm/¼ inch thickness and use to line greased tartlet tins. Prick the base, line with greaseproof paper and fill with dried beans. Bake in the oven at 180°C/350°F/gas mark 4 for 15-20 minutes.

Filling: Beat the 2 eggs with the sugar then add the lemon rind and juice. Pour into a heavy-based saucepan or bain-marie and stir over a gentle heat until the mixture starts to thicken. Add the butter and pour into the tart shells.

Leave to cool then pipe rosette of whipped cream on top of the tarts.

TWELFTH NIGHT ROLL

Serves 8

25g/1oz fresh yeast
75ml/3fl oz milk
550g/1¼ lb flour
125g/4oz lard or butter
25ml/1fl oz rum
grated rind of 1 lemon and 1 orange
1 tsp orange blossom water
40g/1 ½ oz sugar
4 eggs, beaten

Topping:
1 egg, beaten

40g/1½ oz coffee sugar crystals
50g/2oz mixed candied fruit, chopped

These delicious Spanish rolls are traditionally made for children on the "Dia de los Reyes" (Twelfth Night) and like fortune cookies, they contain hidden gifts.

Cream the yeast and milk together in a mixing bowl. Add 100g/14oz of the flour and make a soft dough ball with the fingertips. Cover and leave to rise until doubled in size.

Meanwhile, make a dough with the remaining ingredients by hand or in a food processor. Use no more flour than absolutely necessary. Knead the two doughs together, make a ball, sprinkle with flour and place in a floured bowl. Cover with a cloth and leave to rise for 2-3 hours until doubled in size. Knock back the dough, knead lightly and leave to rise again for 30 minutes.

Knock back and knead again lightly then form into the shape of a ring and place on a greased baking tray. Leave to rise for 30 minutes.

Brush with beaten egg, sprinkle with the sugar crystals and chopped candied fruit and press a "surprise gift" into the base of the dough.

Bake in the oven at 200°C/400°F/Gas Mark 6 for about 30 minutes.

QUICK MARZIPAN

Makes 225g/8oz

100g/4oz icing sugar
100g/4oz ground almonds
2 tsp lemon juice
1 egg white, lightly beaten

Mix the icing sugar and almonds in a bowl. Add the lemon juice and lightly beaten egg white. Beat into a paste and make into a ball.

Place the marzipan ball on a work surface and form into the shape of a rolling pin, using your hands. Wrap in aluminium foil and store in the refrigerator (it will keep for a maximum of 7 days).

To serve, cut into small rounds, or roll out and use as cake covering or cut into individual lengths.

COCONUT COOKIES

Makes 1kg/2.2 lbs

250g/8oz flour
200g/7oz sugar
1 tsp baking powder
125g/4oz butter
4 eggs
250g/8oz desiccated coconut
few drops of vanilla essence
icing sugar

Place the flour, sugar and baking powder in a mixing bowl and mix well. Rub in the butter. Add the eggs one at a time, stirring with a wooden spoon. Flavour with the vanilla essence and add the desiccated coconut. Use the spoon to drop little mounds of mixture onto a greased baking tray. Bake in the oven at 180°C/350°F/Gas Mark 4 for 20 minutes. Remove from the baking sheet and dust with icing sugar.

Top: Quick Mazipan
Bottom: Coconut Cookies

AIRY DOUGHNUTS

Serves 8

75g/3oz butter
pinch of salt
1 tsp sugar
1/4 litre/7fl oz water
125g/4oz flour
4 eggs
oil for frying

Filling:
3 egg yolks
4 tbsp sugar
1 tsp cornflour
grated rind of 1 lemon
1/4 litre/7fl oz boiling milk

Decoration:
icing sugar

The beauty of these doughnuts is that they are completely hollow inside; that is why they are called "airy". The secret is in the way they are fried.

Place the butter, salt, sugar and water in a saucepan and bring to boil. Add the flour all at once and beat until the mixture no longer sticks to the sides of the pan. Remove from heat. Beat in the eggs one at a time (make sure that each egg is well mixed in before adding the next one).

Heat plenty of oil in a large frying pan and before it is too hot, using 2 spoons, drop in little balls of batter the size of a walnut.

The secret is in the temperature of the oil: it must not be too hot, as the doughnuts must first sink in the oil and rise again without browning. When one side has swollen, turn over to allow the other side to swell up. Fry until the doughnuts are golden and have burst open.

Keep the temperature even and fry in batches. When the doughnuts are golden around the crack where they burst, drain well and make a slit in the crack with scissors. Leave to cool, then fill with custard cream and dust with icing sugar.

Filling: Place the egg yolks, sugar and cornflour and grated lemon rind in a saucepan. Pour on the boiling milk and simmer until thickened, stirring constantly. Leave to cool.

ALMOND TILES

Makes about 300g/10oz

125g/4oz sugar
25g/1oz flour
1 egg, beaten

1 egg white, lightly beaten
25g/1oz butter, melted
few drops of vanilla essence
100g/4oz flaked almonds
icing sugar, for dusting

Place the sugar and flour in a mixing bowl, add the beaten egg and egg white and beat in the melted butter with a few drops of almond essence.

Add the almonds, cover and chill overnight. If the dough is too wet, add some ground almonds.

Using a wooden spoon, place little mounds of the mixture onto a greased baking tray. Place them quite far apart to allow room for expansion during cooking. Spread the mounds out with a spatula. Bake in the oven at 200°C/400°F/Gas Mark 6 for 7-8 minutes until golden brown. Remove from the baking tray while hot and bend the biscuits around an empty jar to make then into tile shapes.

Allow to cool and dust with icing sugar.

The thinner the tiles, the more delicious they are.

CHOCOLATE AND ALMOND SNAIL SHELLS

Makes 30

100g/4oz butter
100g/4oz vanilla sugar
1 tsp grated lemon rind
1 egg
200g/7oz flour
Pinch of salt
1 tsp baking powder
50g/2oz ground almonds
1 tbsp cocoa powder

Place the butter in a bowl and beat with an electric mixer until pale and creamy. Add the sugar and lemon rind and continue beating until smooth. Add the egg. Beat thoroughly and add the flour, salt, baking powder and almonds. Mix together to make a dough, then divide the dough in two. Add the cocoa to one half and knead until well mixed in.

Wrap each ball of dough in aluminium foil and chill for 1 hour.

Flour a pastry board or a worktop and roll out the balls into oblongs about 1/2 cm/1/4 inch thick. Place one on top of the other and roll up the two together, swiss-roll style. Wrap in aluminium foil and return to the refrigerator. Chill until very firm.

Cut into 1/2cm thick slices and place the rounds on a greased baking tray. Bake in the oven for 10 minutes at 200°C/400°F/gas mark 6.

CRISPY BONBONS

Makes 1/2kg/1lb

300g/10oz chocolate
75ml/3fl oz single cream
2 tsp brandy
50g/2oz Rice Crispies

Melt the chocolate in a heavy-based saucepan, or bain-marie. Add the cream and brandy and heat for 3 minutes, stirring continuously.

Add the Rice Crispies and stir in quickly so they are coated in chocolate. Allow to cool.

Use a wooden spoon to put little mounds of the mixture onto a greased baking tray. Chill for several hours. Remove from the baking tray with a knife and place each bonbon in a paper petit four case.

Top: Airy Doughnuts
Bottom: Crispy Bonbons

TEA BISCUITS

Makes 1kg/2.2lbs

400g/14oz butter
125g/4oz icing sugar
1 egg yolk
500g/1lb flour

Place the butter in a mixing bowl and beat to a smooth paste. Add the icing sugar and egg yolk. Stir in the flour, first with a wooden spoon, then with the hands. It is best to make this dough quickly without kneading it too much.

Roll out to 1cm/½ inch thickness on a floured work surface. Cut into shapes with a pastry cutter.

Place the biscuits on a baking sheet and bake in the oven at 200°C/400°F/gas mark 6.

Decoration ideas:
1. Brush with beaten egg before baking.
2. Dust with icing sugar after baking.
3. Coat in chocolate hundreds and thousands before baking.
4. Cut out two of each shape, make holes in one and stick together with jam.
5. Coat with glacé icing or apricot glaze.
6. Put a hazelnut, almond or walnut in the middle of each biscuit and brush with egg before baking.
7. Stick two biscuits together with a little melted chocolate, or coat one side with chocolate after baking.

TRUFFLES

Makes 30

350g/10oz plain chocolate
100ml/4fl oz single cream
4 tsp brandy or whisky

Coating:
Cocoa powder
Icing sugar
Praline

Praline:
100g/4oz sugar
75g/3oz nuts (hazelnuts, almonds, walnuts or pistachios)

Melt the chocolate in a mixing bowl placed over a pan of simmering water. Heat the cream in a heavy-based saucepan, add to the chocolate and stir for several minutes. Remove from the heat. Add the brandy or whisky and mix well.

Place the bowl in a bowl of water and ice cubes and beat the mixture vigorously until it lightens and thickens. Chill until set.

Make little balls of the mixture and roll them in cocoa, icing sugar or praline. Place in paper cases and store in the refrigerator to prevent them from becoming soft.

There is also a quicker method to make a large quantity of truffles: Put the truffle mixture in a forcing bag with a straight-edged nozzle and pipe small rosettes onto a sheet of aluminium foil. Freeze for a few minutes, then continue as directed.

Top: Truffles
Bottom: Tea Biscuits

To make the praline, place the sugar in a saucepan, heat until melted then simmer until a golden caramel. Stir in the nuts and pour onto a greased baking tray. Leave to cool then grind to a rough powder.

LANGUE DE CHAT BISCUITS

Makes about ½kg/1lb

125g/4oz butter, softened
125g/4oz sugar
3 egg whites
125g/4oz flour
pinch of salt

Place the butter and sugar in a mixing bowl and stir gently to combine. Add the egg whites one at a time, then the flour and the salt. Chill for 30 minutes.

Place the mixture in a forcing bag with a medium-sized straight nozzle. Pipe small bars of mixture reasonably far apart on a greased baking sheet. Bake in the oven at 170°C/325°F/Gas Mark 3 for 7–8 minutes until the edges are golden.

Remove carefully from the baking sheet and store in a sealed jar. The biscuits will last for a few days.

FRIED MILK BREAD

Serves 6-8

8 slices white bread, crusts removed
225ml/8fl oz milk
8 tbsp sugar
Grated rind of 1 lemon
50g/2oz flour
3 eggs, beaten
50g/2oz fresh breadcrumbs
oil
sugar and cinnamon

Cut the bread slices into quarters. Heat the milk, sugar and lemon rind in a wide saucepan. Dust a large dish with a little of the flour. Using a large slotted spoon, dip each piece of bread in the warm milk then set aside on the dish.

Place the remaining flour on one deep plate, the beaten eggs in another and the breadcrumbs in a third. Heat the oil in a deep medium-sized frying pan. Carefully dip the pieces of bread in flour, followed by egg and breadcrumbs and fry until golden.

Mix the sugar and cinnamon on another plate and coat the fried bread while still hot.

Top: Fried Milk Bread
Bottom: Langue de Chat Biscuits

ORANGE AND LEMON PUNCH CAKE

Serves 6

¼ litre/7fl oz orange juice
¼ litre/7fl oz lemon juice

Sponge:
2 eggs
60g/2½ oz flour
60g/2½ oz sugar
15g/½ oz butter, melted

Meringue:
4 egg whites
200g/7oz sugar

Decoration:
50ml/2fl oz rum
50g/2oz sugar
2 oranges, peeled and sliced
1 lemon, peeled and sliced

To make the sponge, place the sugar and eggs in a mixing bowl and beat together until thick. Add the flour and finally the melted butter. Turn into a greased and floured cake tin and bake in the oven at 190°C/375°F/Gas Mark 5 for 10 minutes.

Grease a fairly deep cake tin and line with slices of the sponge cake.

Freeze the fruit juices. Make a meringue with the sugar and egg whites and beat in the frozen juices. Pour this mixture in the tin lined with sponge and freeze.

Meanwhile, cook the orange and lemon slices with the sugar and rum. When the "sponge punch" is frozen, slice and serve with the cooled fruit mixture.

CHEESE AND QUINCE SQUARES

Serves 6

12 slices Mozzarella cheese
6 oblong Quince Sweetmeats (see page 6)
50g/2oz flour
2 eggs, beaten
150ml/5fl oz oil

Trim the cheese slices to the same size as the sweetmeats. Sandwich each sweetmeat between 2 slices of the cheese. Coat in the flour then the beaten egg and fry until

Left: Orange and Lemon Punch Cake
Opposite: Cheese and Quince Squares

golden. Drain and serve warm with an egg custard.

MILK ROLLS

Makes 25

50g/2oz fresh yeast
100m/4fl oz milk
800g/1³/₄ lb strong white flour
3 eggs,

100ml/4fl oz water
50ml/2fl oz oil
grated rind of 1 lemon and 1 orange
beaten egg, for glazing
sugar, for dusting

Place the yeast in a mixing bowl, warm a few spoonfuls of the milk and blend with the yeast. Add 100g/4oz of the flour and form the mixture into a soft ball. Cover and leave to double in size.

Place the remaining flour in a mould on a working surface. Make a well in the centre and add the eggs, water, oil, grated fruit rind and remaining milk. Mix together with the fingertips then knead until the dough is pliable. When the dough no longer sticks to the fingers, add the yeast mixture. Knead again, greasing the fingertips with oil. Form the dough into a ball, place in a mixing bowl, cover and leave to rise in a warm place for 1½ hours.

Divide the dough into 24 pieces. Form into round rolls, place on a floured baking sheet, cover and leave to rise for 30 minutes. Make a cut down the centre of each roll, brush all over with beaten egg and dust the cut with sugar. Bake in the oven at 200°C/400°F/gas mark 6 for 15-20 minutes until cooked through.

DUTCH PASTRIES

Makes 1kg/2.2 lbs

¹/₂kg/1lb flour
150g/5oz icing sugar
300g/10oz butter, cubed
2 eggs
1 tsp baking powder
¹/₂ tsp vanilla essence
Pinch of salt

Pile the flour on a working surface. Make a well in the centre, add the remaining ingredients and mix with the fingertips to form a smooth dough. Chill for 30 minutes.

Roll out the dough ¹/₂ cm/¹/₄ inch thick on a floured working surface. Cut into different shapes with a pastry cutter, brush with egg white and bake in the oven at 180°C/350°F/gas mark 4 for 20 minutes. Remove before the pastries are too brown.

Allow to cool. Decorate with glacé icing or chocolate glaze and sprinkle with chopped almonds.

Glacé Icing:
Beat together 1 egg white with about 100g/4oz icing sugar and a few drops of lemon juice to form a thick white icing. If desired, half the icing maybe coloured with a drop of red or yellow food colouring.

Chocolate Glaze:
Melt plain chocolate in a bain-marie or microwave. Add some chocolate hazelnut spread and brush over the pastries while still hot.

PRALINE PASTRIES

Makes ½kg/1lb

150g/5oz ground almonds
150g/5oz butter
150g/5oz sugar
100g/4oz flour

Filling:
100g/4oz praline (see below)
100g/4oz butter

Toast the ground almonds and allow to cool. Beat the butter to a paste, add the sugar and continue beating. Mix the flour with the almonds and add to the butter paste. Using a forcing bag with a wide fluted nozzle, pipe flower shapes onto a greased baking sheet. Bake in the oven at 200°C/400°F/gas mark 6 for 5-6 minutes.

Allow to cool and sandwich the pastries together with the praline filling.

Praline filling: place 50g/2oz sugar in a saucepan and heat until melted, then increase the heat and simmer until a golden caramel colour. Add 50g/2oz chopped almonds, pour onto a greased baking tray and allow to cool. Beat the butter to a paste, grind the praline to a rough powder and add to the butter.

PASTRY CIGARETTES

Use the same ingredients and method as for Langues de Chat (page 55). While they are still hot, roll them into a cigarette shape and dip in plain chocolate melted with a knob of butter.

SIMPLE CHOCOLATE CAKES

Makes about 24

100g/4oz plain chocolate
100g/4oz butter
2 tbsp icing sugar
24 sponge fingers, halved lengthways
100ml/4fl oz double or whipping cream

Melt the chocolate in a bain-marie or microwave. Beat the butter to a paste, add the icing sugar and a few spoonfuls of melted chocolate. Leave the remaining chocolate in a bain-marie so it stays liquid. Stir the mixture well to make a creamy paste, then put it into a forcing bag with a medium-sized, fluted nozzle. Place the sponge fingers cut side down in paper cases then pipe on rosettes of the butter mixture.

Place the whipped cream in another forcing bag with a medium-sized, fluted nozzle and pipe flower shapes on top of each cake. Make a small forcing bag from greaseproof paper, pour in the chocolate, snip off the end of the bag and pipe thin patterns over each sponge finger.

MARZIPAN FRUIT SHAPES

225g/8oz sugar
6 tbsp water
170g/6oz ground almonds
50ml/2fl oz liquid glucose
1 egg white, lightly beaten
225g/8oz icing sugar, sifted

Place the sugar and water in a saucepan and heat until the sugar dissolves. Boil without stirring until the syrup is thick. Remove from the heat. Add the almonds and glucose and allow to cool.

When the mixture is lukewarm, add the egg white. Return to a low heat and stir continuously for 2-3 minutes. Add the lemon juice. Remove from the heat and allow to cool, stirring continuously, mixing in the icing sugar a little at a time to form a smooth paste.

Wrap in aluminium foil and chill for up to 7 days until needed.

To make marzipan fruit shapes:
The marzipan may be formed into whatever shape you like. If the dough is slightly dry, add a little more water. Divide the mixture into pieces and add drops of different food colouring to each. For apples or pears, for example, add green food colouring. Shape the marzipan into the desired fruit shapes, using cloves as stems.

To make more realistic bananas, it is best to coat the dough in sugar and bake for a few minutes until golden.

SAN EXPEDITO PASTRIES

Makes 25

1 tsp yeast
225g/8oz strong white flour
1 egg
1 egg yolk
50g/2oz sugar
1 tsp Ricard or Pernod
4 tbsp oil
plenty of oil for frying
icing sugar

Mix the yeast with the flour and place in a mound on a working surface. Make a well in the centre and add the egg, egg yolk, sugar, Ricard or Pernod and oil. Thoroughly mix in the flour with the fin-gertips to form a smooth dough. Knead lightly, form into a ball and set aside to rise for 30 minutes on a greased plate.

Divide the dough into sausage shapes about 7.5cm/3 inches long and fry in oil. The oil is should not be too hot so the pastries can swell with air and cook well inside.

Dust with icing sugar while still hot.

These pastries keep for several days in an airtight tin lined with kitchen paper towels to absorb the oil.

Top: Marzipan Fruit Shapes
Bottom: San Expedito Pastries

CHOCOLATE RINGS

Makes about 36

170g/6oz plain chocolate, broken into pieces
1 tbsp strong black coffee
1 tbsp brandy
75g/3oz butter
25g/1oz sugar
2 egg yolks
1 egg white, lightly beaten
150g/5oz praline (see Praline Pastries on page 58)

Melt the chocolate in a bain-marie or microwave. Add the coffee, brandy, butter and sugar and place in a heavy-based saucepan. Stir over a low heat for a few minutes until well mixed. Remove from the heat and add the egg yolks, beating thoroughly. Chill until firm enough to handle. Turn onto a work surface and form into a 2.5cm/1 inch diameter log. Wrap in aluminium foil and chill again until set.

Unwrap, brush with lightly beaten egg white and coat in praline. If it has softened, chill again until hard.

Wet a knife in hot water, cut the log into ½ cm/¼ inch thick slices and place in paper cases.

Store in the refrigerator.

CHOCOLATE ORANGE FUDGE

Makes 1kg/2.2 lbs

700g/1½ lb sugar
200ml/7fl oz milk
170g/6oz butter
170g/6oz plain chocolate, broken into pieces
grated rind of 1 orange

Grease a shallow rectangular baking tin about 20cm/8 inches long, and line with greased aluminium foil.

Place all the ingredients in a heavy-based saucepan. Stir over a low heat until everything has dissolved and is well mixed. Increase the heat and stir constantly until the temperature reaches 116°C/230°F on a sugar thermometer.

As soon as it reaches boiling point, dip the base of the saucepan in cold water to cool it down. Stir briskly a couple of times to cool, thicken and lighten the colour of the mixture. Pour into the prepared tin and leave to set. Do not refrigerate.

Turn out onto a chopping board, remove the foil and cut into squares or oblongs. May be wrapped in paper or placed in paper cases.

JIJONA TURRON

Makes 2kg/4½ lbs

6 egg whites
400g/14oz toasted, ground almonds
400g/14oz toasted, ground hazelnuts
500g/1lb honey
500g/1lb sugar

In Spain, Turron used to be a special Christmas treat, and every large household had its own recipe. Now it is served all year round. Special oblong wooden moulds are traditionally used in Spain, since the wood allows air to pass through the sides of the mould. Shallow baking trays can be used in place of the moulds.

Line a shallow baking tray with oiled greaseproof paper. Beat the egg whites until stiff and carefully blend in the ground almonds and hazelnuts.

Place the honey in a large saucepan and heat until very runny, then add the sugar. As soon as the sugar dissolves boil until the syrup is thick and will form soft balls when dropped into cold water. Stir the syrup into the egg white mixture and mix well.

Pour the mixture into the prepared baking tray. Cover with oiled greaseproof paper and weigh down. Leave for several days then serve cut into bars.

MARZIPAN TURRON

Makes 2kg/4½ lbs

1kg/2.2 lbs sugar
1 tsp cream of tartar
1kg/2/2 lbs ground almonds
Grated rind of 1 lemon

Place the sugar in a large saucepan with just enough water to cover. Add the cream of tartar and heat to dissolve the sugar, then simmer until syrupy. Test for readiness by dropping a little of the syrup into cold water - it should form threads. Add the ground almonds and grated lemon rind and pour into a shallow baking tray greased with almond oil. Cover with oiled greaseproof paper and weigh down for 4-5 hours. Turn out, cut into small bars to serve.

CADIZ-STYLE TURRON

Makes 2.3kg/5lb

Ingredients and method as for Marzipan Turron

Sprinkle a working surface with icing sugar. Roll out the marzipan to ½cm/¼ inch thickness and cut into oblongs. Place an oblong on rice paper, cut to size, brush with egg yolk, sprinkle on chopped glacé fruit and then place another oblong on top of the fruit layer. Make several thick bars in this way, layering the marzipan bars with egg yolk and fruit. Brush the tops with egg yolk beaten with a little water. Dust with cinnamon and bake in the oven at 200°C/400°F/Gas Mark 6 for 15 minutes until golden.

EGG TURRON

Makes 2kg/4½ lbs

Ingredients and method as for Marzipan Turron

Add 6 egg yolks to the basic almond mixture, beat well, pour into the prepared baking tray and continue as for the basic recipe.

FRUIT TURRON

Makes 2.3kg/5 lbs

Ingredients and method as for Marzipan Turron

Add 225g/8oz chopped, mixed glacé fruit to the basic almond mixture, beat well, pour into the prepared baking tray and continue as for the basic recipe.

Jijona Turron and Marzipan Turron

PLUM CAKE

Makes 1 x 25cm/10 inch cake

125g/4oz currants
125g/4oz sultanas
75ml/3fl oz rum
250g/8oz butter
250g/8oz sugar
4 eggs
250g/8oz flour
2 tsp baking powder
250g/8oz mixed glacé fruit, finely chopped
butter for greasing

Soak the currents and sultanas in the rum for 1-2 hours. Drain well.

Grease a 25cm/10 inch round cake tin and line with greased greaseproof paper.

Place the butter in a bowl and beat with an electric mixer, then add the sugar and continue beating until light and creamy. Add the eggs one at a time, beating well between each egg. Stir in the flour and baking powder. Carefully stir all the fruit into the mixture.

Spoon the mixture into the prepared cake tin and bake in the oven at 160°C/325°F/Gas Mark 3 for about 1½ hours or until a skewer inserted in the centre comes out clean.

Allow to cool, turn out when warm and leave overnight before cutting.

This cake will keep for several days wrapped in aluminium foil.

ALMOND SNAPS

Makes 20

150g/5oz sugar
75ml/3fl oz water
200g/7oz ground almonds
1 egg white
icing sugar

Filling:
150g/5oz sugar
75ml/3fl oz water
1 egg
3 egg yolks

Syrup topping:
4 tbsp sugar
2 tbsp water

Place the sugar and water in a saucepan and heat until the sugar is dissolved. Increase the heat and cook for 5 minutes until thick and syrupy. Add the almonds and stir over the heat until the mixture no longer sticks to the sides of the pan. Remove from the heat, stir in the egg white and mix well. Sprinkle a working surface with icing sugar and roll out the mixture as if it were ordinary dough. Roll on to a rolling pin and cut out 5c x 7cm/2 inch x 3 inch oblongs. Roll them up to resemble brandy snaps, joining the two ends together.

Filling: Make a thick syrup with the egg and water, as above. Beat together the egg and the egg yolks in a heavy-based bain-marie. Pour in the syrup, stirring continuously over the heat. When the mixture no longer sticks to the sides of the pan, place in a forcing bag and pipe into the almond snaps.

Syrup topping: Make a thick syrup with the sugar and water. While it is still hot, brush onto the almond snaps to glaze them. Place on a wire tray and set aside for a few hours. Eat on the same day as making, or they will be too hard.

APPLE FRITTERS

Serves 6-8

4 apples
100g/4oz sugar
75ml/3fl oz rum

Batter:
100g/4oz flour
1 tbsp oil
50ml/2fl oz beer
75ml/3fl oz water
1 egg white, stiffly beaten
dash of rum

Peel and core the apples. Cut into rounds and place in a bowl. Sprinkle with rum and sugar and leave in a cool place for 1 hour.

Batter mix: Combine all the ingredients except for the egg white. Set aside, then just before frying, stir in the stiffly beaten egg white.

Dip the apples in the batter and deep fry in hot oil.

Serve dusted with sugar.

MERINGUE BASKETS

Makes 18

4 egg whites
225g/8oz icing sugar
¼ tsp vanilla essence

Filling:
100ml/4fl oz double or whipping cream
2 tbsp Kirsch
225g/8oz strawberries, raspberries or blackcurrants

To make the meringue, place the egg whites in a mixing bowl over a pan of simmering water and beat until very stiff. Add the icing sugar in two batches and continue beating for 2 minutes. Add the vanilla essence.

Grease a baking sheet and place the meringue in a forcing bag with a medium-sized, fluted nozzle. Pipe onto the baking sheet discs about 5cm/2 inches in diameter, in the shape of small baskets. Dust with icing sugar and bake in the oven at 140°C/275°F/Gas Mark 1 for 1½ hours until the meringue is hard on the outside, but still pale.

The baskets may be made several days in advance.

Fill each basket with strawberries or raspberries in Kirsch and top with whipped cream. Decorate with a single piece of fruit.

If fresh summer fruits are unavailable, substitute frozen fruit or a good quality fruit preserve.

Top: Apple Fritters
Bottom: Meringue Baskets

INDEX